"Provocative, Stimulating, and Convincing: This is an unusual and important book that really delivers on its subtitle: *The Most Convincing Evidence Yet Compiled For The Survival Of Your Soul.* ... even if you know something about the evidence for survival, you will probably learn something new. And if the whole field is something that you've never much thought about, this is an ideal place to start. I hope that this book is widely read; it's implications are stunning. Highly recommended." — Dr. Richard G. Petty, author of *Healing, Meaning and Purpose*

"I found *The Survival Files* to be a well-written, deeply researched, and thought-provoking book. The writing style makes it a hard-to-put-down book." — Captain Robert L. Snow, author of *Looking for Carroll Beckwith*

"Miles Allen has written spiritual material that is both profound and easily understood. For the newcomer to these subjects, it speaks clearly with logic and common sense; for those who have studied over years, it re-confirms and clarifies that which we have long known. A must read." — Dr. Morris Netherton, Director of the Netherton Center for Hypno-Therapy

---

Note: Some of these comments refer to a pre-publication draft of this book, titled *Heaven Confirmed*. Except for minor typographical corrections, the content of both versions is the same.

"This unusual and stimulating book delivers more than its title might suggest ... the twenty-three cases summarised and discussed here are indeed among the best of their kind ... This is an ideal book for absolute beginners, but even advanced students should find something new in it." — Guy Lyon Playfair, review in the *Journal of the Society for Psychical Research*

"I've bought ten copies to give friends, and the response has been unanimously favorable. Everybody has been very impressed; some claiming they just couldn't put it down! I strongly recommend this book to believer's and doubter's alike."
— William Jones, San Jose, CA

"An outstanding accomplishment – The day I received *The Survival Files*, I was busier than usual ... By the time I returned home, it was 10:30 p.m. *The Survival Files* was on the kitchen table and I decided to take a brief look at it. When I next checked the time, it was 3:30 a.m. ... well past my normal bedtime. I got ready for bed and lay there for a quarter of an hour, still considering various issues presented in the book. Although tired, I realized that my desire to continue reading the book had overwhelmed my need to sleep. When, I finished reading the last page of the book, I could see the dawn beginning to peek around the window curtains! ... Mr. Allen has done a masterful job."
— Donald Evans, Depoe Bay, Oregon

"A great book. ... A very interesting, informative, and intriguing read. ... For the person new to psychical research, this book would be an excellent introduction as the various cases are definitely impressive. The author has clearly explored the subject matter and knows how to respond to the debunkers in each case."
— Michael E. Tymn, Book Review Editor, Academy of Spirituality and Paranormal Studies

"I enjoyed *The Survival Files* very much and must admit it introduced me to areas of thought I never before considered. ... A must read for anyone facing a terminal illness, or for any relative or spouse of a person in that condition. If there was ever a book written to allay the fear and dread of dying, this is it!"
— Marge Rieder, Ph.D., author of *Mission to Millboro*

"Allen's approach is insightful, inventive, and carefully reasoned. The information is presented in a flowing dialogue style that is easy to both swallow and digest. Altogether, an enjoyable and memorable read."
— Victor Zammit, author of *A Lawyer Presents The Case For The Afterlife*

THE SURVIVAL FILES

The Most Convincing Evidence Yet Compiled
For The Survival Of Your Soul

Read not to contradict and confute, nor to believe and take for granted, nor to find talk and discourse, but to weigh and consider.
— Sir Francis Bacon, *Of Studies*, 1625

The Survival Files

The Most Convincing Evidence Yet Compiled
For The Survival Of Your Soul

by
Miles Edward Allen

Momentpoint Media

The Survival Files:
The Most Convincing Evidence Yet Compiled
For The Survival Of Your Soul

Published by Momentpoint Media

ISBN: 0-9710448-2-1

Pre-publication drafts of this book
were published under the title
Heaven Confirmed

Cover Design by Miles Edward Allen
Background from photograph by Hubble Spacecraft
of the Dumbbell Nebula - M27,
courtesy of NASA.

In our moments of exaltation,
swept by the sublimity of music or of a sunrise,
we feel that there must be joy at the heart of the universe,
and deep intention;
yet turning again to the harsh realities of life,
with its cruelties and its crushing frustrations,
we cannot but ask,
if we have any perception, any compassion,
any philosophic wonder at all,
the ultimate questions:
What, in the name of sanity,
is the meaning and purpose of life?

— Gina Cerminara, *Many Mansions*, p. 11.

Contents

The old man is fanciful,
the meals are opinion,
the rest is research.

———————————

This book is dedicated to my wife, my best friend, and
my editor — who all reside in Donna's body.

———————————

I would like to recognize all those researchers who have
risked their careers and reputations in the pursuit of truth.
Special thanks to Dr. Raymond Moody, Dr. Morris Netherton, and Dr. Michael Newton for their kind assistance and
advice.

— Miles Edward Allen

Friday Evening

Appalachian Arrival

Seems it strange that thou shouldst live forever?
Is it less strange that thou shouldst live at all?
This is a miracle; and that no more.
— from *Night Thoughts*, by Edward Young

He offered me a drink, but I declined, having been sipping on a Coke for the past two hours as I wound my way to the cabin. I stowed my overnight bag in the loft and followed him out to the screened porch. A gleaming sliver of sun was just vanishing behind the western hills leaving the sky streaked with golden peach and purple.

"So, you want to know about heaven," the old man said, easing down into a well-worn wicker chair "Just why is that?"

"Doesn't everyone wonder what's going to happen next?" I asked, as I pulled my recorder from my pocket, laid it on the slatted top of a small wooden table, and sat down in the rocker beside it.

"Oh, I reckon they do, but not enough to drag their butts all the way out here.

"You were a bit later then I was expecting. Were the directions okay?"

"The directions were fine. No, it's just typical for a Friday before a vacation; everything seems to come to a head an hour before you're due to leave."

"I suppose that's unavoidable," he said. "Trouble is, that feeling tends to stay with us and color our attitude toward life in general; the closer we get to the end, the more pressure we feel to get everything done, wrap it all up in a neat package and, at the same time, we keep thinking of more and more things we really ought to do before we go."

"Yeah, it can get pretty stressful," I said as I stretched my legs out and took a deep breath of forest freshened air. "But you seem to have overcome that problem."

"Being retired and living in beauty certainly helps. But, for me, much of the stress of living disappeared when I became convinced that life never truly ends."

I caught his eye. "You are absolutely certain?"

He turned to look through the screen and, his voice suddenly softer, replied, "I'm as certain that an afterlife exists as I am that there are deer in these hills."

My gaze followed his to the two does stepping carefully between the saplings along the ravine. Dasher, the old man's Chocolate Lab, raised his head from his paws and eyed the deer attentively, but made no sound. We sat still for a while, watching the deer nibbling their way through the misty dusk. A breeze momentarily stirred the leaves, the muffled rustling somehow leaving the woods quieter than silence itself.

I had met him only a few months before during a casino-night charity affair at the New Zealand embassy. My wife and I had volunteered to deal Blackjack. I was taking a break when a fellow I had known well in college waved me over to his group and ordered me a beer and the next thing I knew I was listening to this elderly gentleman speculating as to whether charity was unique to earth or not.

He spoke with such sincerity and authority that the subject didn't seem so strange. His wavy white hair and gunmetal-framed spectacles made him look like Santa Claus in a tux, except his beard was closely trimmed and his round face well-tanned. His name was proffered when he was introduced to me but, since then, I have never heard anyone address him as anything but "sir" or refer to him except as "the old man," so I'll continue that tradition.

After he had strolled off to join another cluster — he seemed to know half of the Washington power brokers in attendance — my friend explained that the man was retired from some arcane but influential post with the State Department and now was preparing to devote his time to lecturing on Survival.[1] My friend suggested that

---

[1] With a capital 'S' it indicates the survival of the human spirit or soul after the death of the body.

I might want to volunteer as a test case (as he already had). Now, I had long been fascinated with the topic and had been toying with book ideas for years, so I did contact the old man and he graciously agreed to share his knowledge. And so I found myself thinking how different he looked tonight, having replaced the tuxedo with a plaid cotton shirt and well-worn jeans.

Impossible to tell how much time passed as thinking gave way to just being there, sitting on an old but comfy rocker in the deepening darkness of the West Virginia hills. Almost heaven? Close enough for me. For the moment.

Finally, I roused myself enough to say, "It's really nice up here. I bet the woods are beautiful in the snow."

"Yep. So long as I have good neighbors with snow plows, it can be real nice here in the winter. You know, the thought of snow makes me realize I'm a bit chilly. How about bringing in a few hunks of wood and we'll have ourselves a fire?"

Indeed, goose bumps on my arms bore witness to the rapid drop in temperature. So I stood and turned off my recorder — just as well, as the only sounds it would have caught for the rest of the night were a few pleasantries amidst the crackle of the fire and then a whole lot of snoring.

Saturday Morning

Other-Body Experiences

If a man can leave his physical body temporarily and continue to exist as a self-conscious being, the fact would prove a strong presumption that eventually when he comes to leave his physical body, i.e., to die, he will then also continue to exist as a self-conscious being in that second body.

— Robert Crookall[2]

"To begin with," he said, after I switched on my recorder, "your readers should know that I am not a medium or a mystic. In fact, I have never had a notable paranormal experience — not in this life anyway. I have simply been an ardent student of psychic phenomena since I was first drawn to it while in college. Over the ensuing decades, I have studied hundreds of books and papers dealing with the evidence for life continuing after death. There is always more to learn, but I feel that my grasp of

[2] Ebon, p. 116.

the subject is sufficient to be of use in teaching others. Also, be aware that I am not associated with any religion. The views I express come only from evidence gathered and facts verified, not from the teachings of any church or organization."

"Duly noted," I said.

"Let's start this morning by focusing on the question: Can mind function independently of matter?

"Ever since the invention of the 'wireless' radio we have thought of long-distance communications in terms of energy traveling between antennae. Television signals, for instance, are electromagnetic pulses that are created by antennae (either on broadcast towers or satellites) and travel outward until they are absorbed by something. When the pulses happen to run into another antenna (such as a satellite dish on the roof of a home) they are converted by a receiver into other signals that, ultimately, create a picture on the TV. All of which is to emphasize the point that communication always involves something being sent from one place, traveling across an intervening space, and then being received at another place."

"Seems sensible enough to me," I said.

"Such is certainly the scientific point of view. Or at least it was until a few decades ago, when physicists studying interactions at the sub-atomic level began to see evidence that information could be exchanged without traversing any intervening distance."

He pulled a book from a high shelf and showed me the cover. "Have you read this?"

I could easily read the large white type atop a photo taken from outer space of the sun peeking over the earth's curved horizon: "Arthur C. Clarke" it read, "The Light of Other Days."[3]

"Clarke is one of my favorite science-fiction authors," I replied, "but I didn't know he wrote a book about near-death experiences."

"Yes, the cover does suggest that, doesn't it. So many NDE books use 'the light' in their titles. But, no, this book is an examination of what might happen if scientists actually managed to establish and control wormholes."

"Wormholes are sort of tunnels through space-time, right? They're what fictional space ships use to get from one galaxy to another without having to spend a gazillion years crossing the intervening distance. You just sort of pop into one end and promptly pop out the other."

"Only Clarke doesn't push the science hard enough to have people and ships traveling through the wormholes — just light and sound. Of course, the equipment needed to observe other places and times is huge and superbly expensive ... at first. As with the development of most technologies, however, it gets smaller and cheaper and, in a remarkably short

---

[3] Co-authored by Stephen Baxter, published by Tom Doherty Associates, 2000.

time, as the story is told, every kid on the block has a 'worm cam' on his or her wrist with which to view any action that is occurring or has occurred at any place in the universe at any time throughout history."

"That would mean an absolute end to privacy," I mused.

"As well as an end to crime, not to mention a lot of revising of history," he added, "and the book does a respectable job of exploring what all that means for society. But I didn't bring it up so we could fantasize about being the ultimate voyeurs, rather because it provides a good way to introduce the subject of viewpoints.

"The trans-dimensional tunnel known as a wormhole has, like any other tunnel, two ends. One end is where the tunnel is created, at the worm cam. The other end, known as the 'mouth' is at the point in space/time that the operator desires to observe. According to the book, this mouth can be opened anywhere, from the inside of a closet, to the inside of a person, to the inside of a star. But — now pay close attention because this is the point that I went through all this to make — but, the mouth must be opened *somewhere*."

"That," I observed, feeling a bit unsure of the route we seemed to be taking, "seems fairly obvious."

"Obvious, yes, but also very easy to forget.

"Now, pretend for a moment that you own one of these nifty devices and you decide to check up on a friend of yours who is undergoing surgery at a local hospital. You find yourself a quiet, comfortable place where you won't be interrupted for a while, slip on the headset (which gives you a three-dimensional, totally realistic image) and dial in the coordinates of the operating theater. You click the 'go' button and with only a split-second of disorientation, you seem to be above the operating table. From here you can see a film of dust on the top of the floodlights. You can see the tops of the heads of the doctors and nurses. You can see, and hear, everything within the room exactly as if you were actually hovering near the ceiling.

"You aren't familiar with the surgical procedures, but you note that everyone is calm so you assume that all is going well. Then, suddenly, there is a power failure and all the lights go out. Being in a windowless room, you can see nothing, although you can hear the surgeon curse. It only takes a moment, though, for the emergency power to kick in and order is restored. After a while, you begin to wonder what else might be happening at the hospital. Back in the room where your body reposes, your fingers tweak the worm-cam controls and the mouth of the tunnel shifts out into an adjoining corridor. To your eyes it seems that you have floated effortlessly through a wall and are now watching people moving along the hallway."

Turning to replace the book on the shelf, he asked, "What if you wanted to read the model number printed on a sticker underneath the table?"

"Well, I suppose I would use my worm-cam controls to move back through the wall and position the tunnel's mouth beneath the table so that I could look up at the sticker."

"And what if you wanted to read the numbers stamped on the electrical box holding the light switches inside the wall?"

"I don't know," I replied. "If I couldn't see the room in the darkness of the power outage, how could I see inside a wall where there would be no light? Unless this worm-cam has infra-red capabilities. That might enable viewing of the number."

"An excellent point," he offered an approving smile. "Now go back down the hall to a small waiting area. On the table is a stack of magazines. Read me what is written on page seven of the third magazine from the top."

"Whoa! Unless someone picks up the magazine and opens it to pages six and seven, I don't think I can do that. Even if I could precisely position the mouth of the tunnel between pages six and seven, I not only would have no light to see by, but I wouldn't have the necessary perspective. I mean, in real life I can't read with my eyeball pressed up against the page. If I back away from the page to get sufficient perspective, then the other pages would be in my way."

"Precisely."

"And, now that I think of it," I continued, "it's also a question of focus. If I get too close to something in real life my eyes can't focus on it. Just how do you focus one of these worm cams anyway?"

"I'm afraid the authors forgot to explain that little trick," he lamented.

"Well, I'm no optician, but I know a little something about photography and I know that if you try to take a picture with no lens on the camera the result will be an indecipherable blob. Without a lens at the opening of the wormhole, all the light rays coming from all directions in the room will enter in a totally incoherent jumble and there would be no way to clarify the picture at the other end of the tunnel."

"So, we have deduced several requirements for viewing at a distance with a worm-cam. First, you need to have light, then you need to have a lens to focus the light rays, and finally, you need to be able to position the lens so as to provide the proper angle of view and perspective of the subject. Furthermore — and this may seem obvious, but it is an important distinction — if you want to change views you must move the lens."

"Hey," I quipped, "it's good to know that if such a thing as a worm cam is ever invented we'll be ready."

The old man grinned and went on, "Let's see if our newly considered knowledge is of any use as we take up the subject of clairvoyance, out-of-body experiences, astral travel, remote viewing, and near-death experiences."

"I never thought of all those as being the same subject."

"Well, let's find out. What is clairvoyance?"

"Literally, it means clear seeing," I replied. "The term indicates the ability to view objects and events that are beyond the normal range of sight."

"And how would this differ from remote viewing?"

"When various federal offices began experimenting with psychic spying, I guess they felt that 'clairvoyance' sounded too flaky for government work, so some bureaucrat came up with the term 'remote viewing'. A few ex-agents like to think of remote viewing as being a structured and systematic process as compared to the more casual clairvoyance, but it seems to me that they're just different names for the same thing."

"Okay. How about OBEs and astral travel?" he asked.

"'OBE,' or 'OOBE,' is an acronym for Out-Of-Body Experience. 'Astral' is an older term that refers to an alternate reality that supposedly exists in the same space as our physical world but at a different vibratory level. 'Astral travel' means pretty much the same thing as 'OBE' except that it implies the existence of an astral body in which one can traverse the astral world."

"So, one doesn't require any sort of ethereal body to have an OBE?"

I thought for a while and replied: "During an OBE, people report the sensation of leaving their physical body, but they seem to exist as a localized energy body of some sort. If this were not true, then it wouldn't be an OBE, it would simply be clairvoyance. It would probably be more accurate to have 'OBE' stand for <u>Other</u>-Body Experience."

"You know, it probably would," he agreed. "Let's use that term from now on and see how it works out.

"So, if I'm sitting in a room and a vision comes to mind of something happening at a distant place, that would be clairvoyance. But if I have the feeling of traveling in my 'other body' to that distant place and witnessing that event and then returning to my physical body, that would be an OBE?"

"I guess so."

"The difference, then, between an OBE and clairvoyance is really a matter of the psychological perspective of the percipient — whether or not one has the sensation of leaving their physical body."

"Are you saying that one doesn't actually leave their body during an OBE?" I asked.

"On the contrary," he said, and said no more.

After a moment, I got his point. "We're back to the worm cam, aren't we?"

He only raised an eyebrow, so I continued. "And back to the TV antennae.

"In order to perceive something, there has to be a signal sent and received. Even if the distance between sender and receiver can be eliminated via an extra-dimensional jump, the reception of a picture still requires the existence, at the observed site, of a lens of some sort located at such a point as to have the necessary viewing angle and focus to capture the scene in perspective. This is just as true in cases of so-called 'clairvoyance' as in out-of ... I mean *other*-body experiences.

"Which suggests, I suppose, that clairvoyance, remote viewing, and astral travel are all actually cases of other-body experiences — sometimes with a sense of 'being there' and sometimes without."

"Okay," he agreed, "let's go on that assumption, at least for the moment."

"But NDEs are a different thing all together. Aren't they?"

"In total, they are," he said. "The near-death experience typically has several stages — the dark tunnel, the life review, the brilliant light, the overwhelming love, and the decision to return, being common ones. But virtually all NDEs begin with an OBE. The 'dying' person experiences the world as if he or she were hovering above their physical body. This stage of the NDE seems no different than the other-body experiences of healthy folks.

"Most of the OBEs that I think are particularly convincing were reported as part of NDEs. This is because NDEs are more likely to be witnessed and be better documented than other OBEs, which are typically spontaneous and generally lack supporting testimony.

"This is a copy of my current collection of best evidence for the continuation of personal identity after physical death," he said, taking down a sky-blue, wire-bound manual and handing it to me.

I opened it. The title page said: *An Afterlife Casebook: Extraordinary Evidence for Extraordinary Claims*.

"Go ahead," he urged, "read the first case. I'll make us some tea."

"Make mine iced if you would," I said and began to read.

Case 1— Seattle Shoe

When Maria had her first heart attack she was visiting friends in Seattle, not gathering crops in some field far removed from quality medical assistance. Even migrant workers get lucky now and then. Perhaps just as fortunate as the high-caliber cardiac care afforded Maria at Harborview Medical Center was the compassionate attention she received from the social worker in the coronary care unit. Kimberly Clark, M.S.W., was exceptionally empathic, with a knack for calming and reassuring folks who had every reason to be upset. She soon put Maria's mind at ease about family and finances and Maria came to see her as a trusted friend in a strange place.

This became evident on the fourth day, after Maria went into cardiac arrest for a second time. She was resuscitated by the medical team and seemed to be okay, but upon regaining consciousness later in the day, she became so agitated that the nurse on duty was afraid she would give herself another heart attack. Clark was called and, with considerable effort, managed to calm Maria down sufficiently to hear her story.

Maria said that after her attack that morning she had found herself floating near the ceiling of her room, watching the resuscitation procedures. She described those in the room, the things they did, and the equipment they used. After a while, she claimed, she found herself outside of the hospital building, where she noted the location and design of the emergency entrance.

Even though everything Maria said was accurate, Clark admits that she refused to believe her. "I knew the essential facts Maria was relating — the setting, the sequence of events — were true. But my professional, rational mind told me that Maria was 'confabulating,' that she was unconsciously filling in the blanks of her memory"[4] Clark felt that Maria must have gotten the details right "due to information she had somehow been privy to," although she had no idea how.

Then Maria dropped the bombshell that would reverberate throughout the NDE community for decades to come. She claimed that something on a ledge outside the building had drawn her attention and that then she found herself about three stories above the ground staring at a single shoe. It was a man's dark-blue tennis shoe, well-worn, one lace caught under the heel. The shoe was scuffed, Maria said, on the left side, where the

---

[4] For the full story, see pages 3 - 16 of *After the Light* by Kimberly Clark Sharp.

little toe would be. Then Maria looked expectantly at Clark.

"It was clearly up to me," Clark reports, "to look for the shoe." Thinking that it might make Maria feel better to know that someone trusted her, Clark set off on what she was sure would be a "futile search." First she went outside and walked around the entire building. All she gained was an appreciation for the enormity of the Harborview complex. Nothing could be seen on any window ledge. Then, despite it being past quitting time, she felt impelled to do a room-to-room inspection on the third floor. "From the rooms on the east side, I saw nothing," she recalls. "On the north side — nothing. I was four rooms into the west side of the building when I pressed my face against a window pane, peered down on yet another ledge, and felt my heart go *thunk*. There it was."

Clark couldn't see if there was a worn area on the little toe because that side was away from her, but all the other details coincided perfectly with Maria's description. She opened the window and picked up the shoe. Yes, the scuff mark was also as described.

Maria was so excited when she saw the shoe that the monitoring nurse came in to see why her heart rate had jumped so high. Clark and Maria told the nurse what had happened. "By the next morning," Clark relates, "every nurse in the CCU knew Maria's story, and by afternoon, a parade of doctors and nurses and other staff members had dropped in to pay their respects to the humble shoe."

End Case 1

When I finished reading, I thanked him for the tea and said: "Some of this story seems familiar. I think I've read about it before, but I didn't realize it was so convincing."

"It has been quoted — and misquoted — in many publications, so your sense of familiarity is understandable. What do you find so convincing about it?"

"Well, I guess it isn't really proof of Survival, since Maria didn't have much time to 'live' after she 'died.' And she really only 'died' in a technical sense, if at all, since she lived to tell the tale. But this is very strong evidence that some kind of 'astral body' (for want of a better term) exists and can operate at least semi-independently of the physical body.

"Would I be safe to assume that the report of this incident has drawn considerable fire from the skeptics?"

"A true Skeptic (in the philosophical sense) doesn't have a position and won't take a position," he pointed out.

"You know who I mean," I contended, "those debunkers and fanatical critics who have made a career out of denying psychic phenomena."

"Yes, I know." he admitted. "Perhaps we should call them 'super skeptics' or maybe 'überskeptics' would be more appropriate."

"This world does host some perplexing people."

"Well, it's understandable. We all want the security of being part of the pack, but we also want to stand out from it and feel special in some way. Perhaps this is why some people seem driven to denigrate any commonly held belief. As far back in history as we can discern, most people have believed in the continuation of personality beyond the death of the body. Even though believing in something doesn't make it so, the near universality of belief in an afterlife should at least confer a predisposition to seriously evaluate evidence, even what may, at first, seem incredible.

"Those who refuse to be objective tend to stay away from the truly evidential cases. I guess they just don't want to draw any more attention to incidents that undermine their position. For the most part, überskeptics prefer to make general statements dismissing all such cases as the result of either prior knowledge or lucky guesses.

"Those few who do mention Maria's case act as if it has been discredited by an article that was once published in the *Skeptical Inquirer*."[5]

"Where else?" I muttered, rather sarcastically.

---

[5] Ebbern, pp. 27-33.

"If you think of that magazine as biased against psi, this article, written by a few students from Simon Fraser University, isn't likely to change your opinion. In it, the students claim that they visited Harborview and managed to place a shoe on the ledge so that it could be seen easily from inside the room. This, they state, indicates that someone saw the shoe and then proceeded to discuss it within earshot of Maria. The students conclude that Maria must have overheard these comments about the shoe and incorporated them into her dying dream."

"But all that really proves," I noted, "is that it was *possible* for the students to place the shoe in a visible spot. Clearly, this was *not* the spot where Clark says she could see the shoe only by pressing her face against the window. So, by making this argument, the students have managed to challenge Clark's credibility without explicitly claiming that she made up the entire story."

"You might say that.

"You might also take note of the fact that (according to their story) even for the shoe that the students placed in such a visible spot, the details of the worn toe and lace placement would not have been visible unless the observer 'pressed against the glass.' In summary then, we are being asked by the students to believe that someone noticed a tennis shoe on the widow ledge, pressed his or her face against the glass to see that the far side of the shoe had a worn spot on the little-toe area and that a lace was tucked up under the heel. This person, we are asked to believe, was so impressed by these wondrous details that he later related all of them to another person while in the presence of a deathly ill woman in a different area of the hospital. But, at the same time, this person *was not* sufficiently impressed to bother to open the window and retrieve the proof of this strange occurrence, and so left the shoe for someone else to discover.

Furthermore, when Maria's experience became the talk of the hospital, neither the shoe's discoverer nor the person to whom he told the tale, nor any of the many people who must have seen this 'obvious' shoe on the ledge prior to Clark retrieving it, ever came forward to claim his or her due notoriety."

"I can see why most skepti ... überskeptics are reluctant to cite that article," I said. "Nevertheless, if this was the only case with hard evidence of the existence of a conscious 'other body,' I might be tempted to accept their explanation, no matter how preposterous. After all, unlikely events do sometimes happen.

"But I suspect your interest in OBEs isn't built on a single case."

He nodded toward the blue manual beside me. "Take a look."

Case 2 — Dutch Dentures

On 15 December 2001, the international medical journal, *The Lancet*, published a report titled "Near-death experience in survivors of cardiac arrest: a prospective study in the Netherlands."[6] This study included 344 patients who were successfully resuscitated after cardiac arrest. Of the 62 patients who reported some sort of an experience, 15 claimed that they had left their body. This is 24 percent of those who had an experience of some sort, and 4.4 percent of the total patients resuscitated.

Those who claimed some sort of an NDE were interviewed soon after their experience and again 2 years and 8 years later. Of special interest is what the report terms "a surprising and unexpected finding" that the positive, life-changing effects of the NDEs, rather than fading with time, became more and more apparent as the years passed.

This is by far the largest study of its kind and it sheds a great deal of light on the NDE process. All those critics who have managed to ignore such veridical evidence as "Maria's shoe" and have assumed that NDEs are hallucinations caused by a lack of oxygen or the administration of drugs need to take note of the chief investigator's conclusion: "Our results show that medical factors cannot account for the occurrence of NDEs."

Part of the *Lancet* report is the testimony of a coronary-care-unit nurse telling of a night when a comatose man was brought in by ambulance. During

---

[6] Vol. 358, 15 December 2001, pp. 2039-42. A good overview of the study in layman's terms is available at www.iands.org/dutch _study.html.

treatment, his mouth is opened to insert a breathing tube and it is discovered that he is wearing dentures. These are removed by the nurse reporting the incident and placed in a drawer of a crash cart. After about an hour of treatment the patient is transferred to the intensive care unit, still in the comatose condition in which he arrived.

The nurse does not see this patient for more than a week, then she meets him in the cardiac ward. In her own words (translated, of course, from the Dutch): "The moment he sees me, he says: 'Oh, that nurse knows where my dentures are.' I am very surprised. Then he elucidates: 'Yes, you were there when I was brought into the hospital and you took my dentures out of my mouth and put them into that cart, it had all those bottles on it and there was this sliding drawer underneath and there you put my teeth.' I was especially amazed because I remember this happening when the man was in deep coma and in the process of CPR."

The nurse inquired further and the man told her that he had seen himself lying on the bed while the staff had performed CPR. He correctly described the room he had been in and the appearance of the staff members present. She concludes: "He is deeply impressed with his experience and says he is no longer afraid of death."

End Case 2

He saw me look up from the book and spoke: "Let me tell you why I think that is a very impressive case."

"Okay," I said, keeping my finger at my place and resting the book in my lap.

"One of the favorite tactics of the NDE debunker is to point out that hearing is the last sense to fail as a dying brain's activity declines. And, it is true that people under anaesthesia have sometimes reported hearing conversations among surgical staff during operations. So, it is claimed that many, if not all, NDE/OBEs are hallucinations based upon sounds made by people and equipment as consciousness shuts down. Indeed, this might explain some OBEs and some part of many NDEs, but it certainly does not account for most NDEs. And this is an excellent example of one that is unaccounted for.

"There is no mention of any sound accompanying the placing of the dentures in the drawer, but let's assume that the nurse actually announced 'I'll put his dentures in this drawer.'"

"Not very likely," I interjected. "Especially in the emergency room frenzy."

"Yes, but even if she described her actions over the public-address system, the man had no way of knowing *who* was taking his teeth. In the unlikely event that his coma allowed for some hearing, his eyes — at least his *physical* eyes — certainly were not functioning. Yet he knew that the drawer was 'underneath' the cart, and, most importantly, he recognized this nurse as the teeth taker 'the moment' he saw her again, before she had a chance to speak."

"I see your point," I said, "and I certainly feel more comfortable accepting the shoe story now that I know it doesn't stand alone."

"Oh, there are many such veridical stories. Curiously, at least two other good cases involve shoes![7] But, I'm particularly fond of the next one, which also involves hospital procedures and a nurse."

"Maybe you just have a thing for nurses," I joked. But he barely smiled and so I flipped the book open.

Case 3 – The Cavalier Nurse

Dr. Raymond Moody, philosopher, psychiatrist, and author of the best-selling *Life After Life*, relates an incident[8] in which he was attempting to resuscitate an elderly woman. While he was giving her closed-heart massage, a nurse on duty in the emergency room hurried into an adjoining storage area to get some medication he needed. This was packaged in a glass vial that was intended to be opened by snapping the thin neck with one's fingers. Protocol called for protecting the fingers by wrapping the vial in a paper towel. Upon her return, the nurse handed Moody the vial open and ready for use.

---

[7] Ring, *Lessons from the Light*, pp. 67-69.

[8] Moody, *The Light Beyond*, pp. 19-20.

When the woman regained consciousness, she looked directly at the nurse and admonished: "Honey, I saw what you did, and you're going to cut yourself doing that."

The astonished nurse confessed that she didn't want to take the time to find a paper towel, so she had broken the vial with her bare fingers.

End Case 3

"I was wondering when we were going to get to Moody," I said, "after all he is the father of the near-death experience."

"Well, Moody coined the term, but he would be the first to point out that the experiences have been reported at least as far back as Plato. Moody does deserve our respect and admiration for risking his career by publishing the book that triggered most of the research into NDEs. It's hard to imagine now, but prior to 1975, unless you had undergone the experience yourself, you probably hadn't heard of it.

"What do you think of his story?"

"It's short but neat," I said. "And it beautifully counters the idea that patients extrapolate their OBEs from sounds they overhear while comatose. It is extremely unlikely that anyone, even if they were awake and possessed exceptionally sharp hearing, could detect the snapping of a glass vial in a room adjoining a noisy emergency room. It is even less likely that a comatose person, whose chest was being urgently pounded, could properly interpret the meaning of such a minute click. The idea that someone could do all that *and* discern whether the vial was held by bare or paper-towel-covered fingers is so preposterous ... well, I'd sooner believe that all toys are made at the North Pole by tiny elves."

"I take it, then, that you are convinced of the reality of the NDE/OBE?"

"I'm convinced that something is happening that is unexplainable in terms of materialism or scientism. But I'm not ready to commit to any new theory."

"Let's give Dr. Moody another opportunity then, shall we? The next case is what he calls his "most dramatic story." He related it to me in recent conversations.[9] The subject was his neighbor and friend whom he considered "the salt of the earth.""

Case 4 — The Plaids and the Pallbearer

June[10] was in her mid-30s when she elected to undergo what was supposed to be routine gall-bladder surgery. The routine was shattered when her heart stopped beating. As the doctors were attempting to resuscitate her, June sensed herself rising from her physical body and moving out into a hospital corridor where she encountered a few of her friends and family members who had gathered quickly. (The hospital was

---

[9] In March and April of 2005.

[10] Parts of June's story were related (as two separate incidents) in *The Light Beyond*. Her name has been changed in deference to her family's privacy.

within a short walk of their home in northeastern Alabama.) She attempted to attract their attention but failed. Her strongest memory of the group is that her daughter was dressed in mismatched plaids.

Moving on down the corridor, June came upon her brother-in-law. As she was attempting to communicate with him, a friend of his happened along and asked him why he was there. In answer, she heard her brother-in-law say that he had intended to visit an uncle who lived out-of-town, but now he thought he should stick around because June was going to "kick the bucket" and he might be needed as a pallbearer.

Next, June found herself having a typical NDE-tunnel experience at the end of which she encountered two translucent beings, one of whom was an infant. To her inquiry as to their identity, the infant peeled back his outer covering as one might take off a bathrobe and transformed into an adult male. "I am your brother," he stated. As far as June knew, she only had sisters.

Upon regaining consciousness, June discussed these events with her family and discovered that they all checked out. Her father confessed that his first child was a boy who died within a few days of birth and was never mentioned within the family. Her brother-in-law confirmed that he had been standing apart from the others when his friend came along and he sheepishly admitted to making the remark about being a pallbearer. And, when questioned about the mismatched plaids, June's maid said that in her rush to get the family to the hospital, she had grabbed the top two items in the daughter's laundry basket (not heeding their patterns) and told her to get dressed.

June's testimony was confirmed independently in interviews Dr. Moody held with June's surgeon, her father, her brother-in-law, and her maid.

End Case 4

"Most dramatic indeed! This case would be very tough to explain by any means other than actual travel in the other body."

"Give it a try," he prompted.

"Well, I suppose she could have learned that she had a brother without being conscious of the fact, but goodness knows that would be a strange way to reveal it to herself. And why bother at such a critical time in her life? Having a male sibling could hardly have an impact on whether she lived or died."

"But, however improbable, you are right to point out that unconscious knowledge is a possible explanation for the brother incident."

"Then," I continued, "I guess June could have read the mind of her brother-in-law to learn of his remarks about being a pallbearer."

"An excellent point," he said, "although überskeptics deny the possibility of mind reading. Also, that doesn't explain how June knew he was down the hall from the rest of the family when his friend approached him."

"No, nothing does, except clairvoyance, and we agreed that's just another kind of OBE. The same thing goes for her daughter's clothes. You know," I mused, "I'm sure that I'll forget many of the particulars I learn this weekend, but I'll never shake the image of that little girl in those mismatched plaids."

"Then I bet you'll appreciate the story about the woman who didn't believe there was a heaven. When she had an NDE, she was very upset to discover the reality of an afterlife, for she never liked to be proven wrong. Furthermore, during her OBE she noticed that she had been dressed in a nightgown that didn't match her robe and she was furious to think that she would have to spend eternity in mismatched clothing!"

"That's a good one," I chuckled. "I didn't know you had comedic aspirations."

"Oh, that's not a joke," he replied. "It's from a collection of actual cases about the impact of NDEs on those who don't believe in heaven.[11]

"Anyway, if there's a more evidential OBE story than June's, I haven't heard it. At least as far as adults are concerned. Now let's look at what the younger ones have to say about OBEs."

I took my cue to resume reading.

---

[11] Cox-Chapman, pp. 134-135.

Case 5 — Room Reconnoiter

Rick was an adult when he related his story to Dr. Melvin Morse,[12] but it began when he fell deathly ill at the age of 5. He remembers leaving his body and watching the medics carrying him out of his house, loading his body into the ambulance and driving away. But, atypically, he didn't follow his body in the ambulance. Instead, he stuck around long enough to see his father weeping as his family got into their car to go to the hospital. Then, he claims: "I went ahead to the hospital to see what kind of room I was going to get. I saw a girl who was about 12 years old in the room that I was supposed to go into. Since I was so sick, they decided to move her and give me the room alone."

Following this observation, Rick continued with a more typical experience involving a tunnel and a bright light. The light was all knowing and all loving, but he knew that if he entered it he could not return to his family.

When Rick came out of his coma several days later, his family was astounded to hear that he knew about his father's tears and about the girl being moved from his room prior to his (body's) arrival at the hospital.

End Case 5

---

[12] Morse, pp. 177-179.

"The bit about the girl being transferred to another room makes for an interesting twist to the story," I said. "But that is the kind of thing that might have been mentioned in the presence of the comatose boy."

"True enough," he replied, "and the father's tears?"

"Probably not mentioned, but easy enough to guess. Although I hesitate to impugn the testimony of a young child with no apparent motive to make up a story. It's also tough to imagine that a 5-year-old was so culturally indoctrinated as to fabricate the tunnel and the loving light. No, all together, the story adds to the evidence of Survival. Nevertheless, I'd much prefer to hear such testimony sooner than two decades after the event occurred."

"Your wish is my command."

Case 6 – From the Mouths of Babes

There are many hundreds of accounts, such as the one cited in Case 5, in which adults recall having NDEs as children; the following are highlights from some of the rarer instances in which children have provided evidence of NDEs while they are still children, thus minimizing any possible distortion over time.

The first is from a study published by pediatrician Melvin Morse in 1986, the rest from other sources as cited.[13]

June, at the age of 8 — gets her hair caught in a swimming pool drain and her heart stops for 45 minutes. A few months later, during a medical interview, June tells of floating above her body, going up a tunnel, and visiting a bright and cheerful place where "a nice man asked me if I wanted to stay."

Sam, at the age of 8 — suffers cardiac arrest as a result of an adrenal gland disease. As a 9-year-old undergoing a routine medical exam, he suddenly, and somewhat shyly, tells the doctor: "About a year ago, I died." Encouraged to elaborate, he tells of floating above his body and trying unsuccessfully to stop a doctor from hitting him on the chest. Then he flew quickly into the sky and through a tunnel to a place where he met glowing angels (without wings). There he

---

[13] June's story is reported in *Closer to the Light* by Melvin Morse, p. 37. Sam's story is reported in *The Light Beyond*, by Raymond Moody, pp. 58-59. Mike's story is reported in "Pediatric Death Experiences" by William J. Serdahely in the *Journal of Near Death Studies*, vol 9, no. 1, Fall 1990, pp. 33-41. José's story is reported in *Lessons from the Light* by Kenneth Ring, pp. 105-6. Todd's story is reported in *With the Eyes of the Mind: An Empirical Analysis of Out-of-Body States*, by Glen O. Gabbard, p. 156. Nathan's story is reported by his mother at http://members.tripod .com/celestialtravelers/nat.html. Charlotte's (a pseudonym I assigned) story is reported in "Near-Death Experiences in the Very Young," by Herzog and Herrin, in *Critical Care Medicine*, vol. 13, 1985, p. 1074.

saw a fence and knew that if he crossed it he could not return to his life. He wanted to stay there, he claimed, but God made him go back.

Mike, at the age of 4 — falls from a high dive and lands on his head. His mother finds him and thinks he is dead. When he regains consciousness he tells her that he was floating out of his body and then a shaft of yellow light surrounded him. Then he heard a voice asking him if he wanted to live or die and, thinking of his mother, he decided to live.

José, at the age of 3 years, 8 months — almost drowns and spends the next 2 weeks in a coma. At the age of eleven, without any prompting, he tells his mother that he remembers having risen into the air and seeing her and his father crying. Then he met people he liked who shone very brightly. He felt good and wanted to stay with these people but they told him he could not.

Todd at the age of 2 years, 8 months — is asked by his mother if he remembers what happened 4 months earlier when he was almost electrocuted by biting into an electrical cord. (Todd had no heartbeat or respiration for at least 25 minutes.) He replies that he went into a room that had "a very bright light in the ceiling" and that "a very nice man … asked me if I wanted to stay there or come back to you."

Nathan, at the age of 7 months — is operated on for a collapsed intestine. The surgeons report that they "almost lost him." When Nathan is 2 years old, he starts drawing pictures of a person in a beam of yellow light beneath a rainbow. In answer to his mother's query as to why he keeps drawing the same picture, Nathan replies that he is drawing himself so he can remember the time he went up in the sky. Then he says, "Remember when I was a baby and I hurt so bad? I went up in the yellow light and through a rainbow and I didn't hurt any more. There were people there that told me I had to go back because you and dad still needed me."

Charlotte, at the age of 6 months — was hospitalized for severe renal and circulatory failure. Against the expectations of the doctors, she survived. At the age of 3½, as her mother was speaking of the impending death of her grandmother, Charlotte asked: "Will Grandma have to go through the tunnel to get to see God?"

End Case 6

"Whew! This is some very touching stuff." I paused a while to figure out my feelings.

"The stories are both heartwarming and heartrending. I mean, I have friends who have lost young children. I'm sure they'd appreciate any evidence that those children's souls survived death ..."

"But?"

"But ... Well, these stories do support the idea of Survival, but they're actually about children who were saved. The heartrending questions are 'Why aren't they all saved?' and 'Did my child make the choice to leave?'"

"Certainly, many children are so badly injured or dissipated that their physical bodies cannot be repaired," he said sadly. "As for making choices, well I don't have good statistics, but I have read a whole lot of these cases and my impression is that the question about staying or returning is more of a survey than a decision point. As with the case of 'Sam', it often doesn't seem to be up to the children, even when they are asked. So, no matter how lovely heaven seems or how pleasant it feels, I doubt that any child stays there if it is physically possible to return to a loving family.

"Any other observations?"

"These accounts are pretty strong evidence that NDEs are not the result of cultural indoctrination. Last I heard anyway, Fisher-Price hadn't created a line of crib toys with tunnels leading to heaven. And, in the accounts given, its clear that the kids weren't trying to satisfy an authority figure who was asking leading questions. What was this Morse study you mentioned?"

"Dr. Morse compared 121 children who had serious diseases (but were never in danger of dying) with 12 children who had clinically died or had been very close to dying. All of the very sick group had been bedridden for extensive periods, and most had been heavily medicated, yet, in intensive interviews, not a single one of them reported experiencing anything like an NDE during their hospital stay. Of the twelve who had knocked on death's door, however, ten reported experiencing at least two elements common to NDEs and seven (58 percent) remembered having an OBE while the doctors were trying to resuscitate them.

"Dr. Morse was careful not to ask directly about OBEs or tunnels or any such common NDE element. His questions were phrased in general terms such as 'Did you have any dreams or do you remember being unconscious?' Also, he did not solicit experiencers nor did he accept volunteers; instead, he methodically went through 10 years of hospital records and interviewed every child who survived a near-fatal illness.[14] So his data isn't distorted by folks anxious to tell — and possibly exaggerate — their tales.

"In that case," I concluded, "the argument for the authenticity of OBEs is further strengthened. Do you have more on the subject?"

"I think we've looked at a pretty representative sampling of the OBEs that provide the best evidence for the existence of a non-physical body. Of course, for every case with verifiable observations there are at least a thousand cases that lack such details."

"Which means," I interjected, "that they could be hallucinations of a dying brain, as critics are wont to claim."

"If you can figure out how a brain with no detectable electrical activity manages to have complex

---

[14] Morse, pp. 21-22.

hallucinations and then manages to store the memories thereof, you could be right.

"Unless, of course, you count the OBEs reported by people who are blind," he said, motioning once more to the book in my lap.

Case 7 – Seeing Is Believing

In the early 1990s, Kenneth Ring, Professor Emeritus of Psychology at the University of Connecticut, partnered with Sharon Cooper (then a Ph.D. candidate at New York University) to undertake the first systematic study of NDEs and OBEs in blind persons. Ultimately they found and interviewed 31 persons who reported either an NDE or an OBE or both. Of these, 14 had been blind since birth, 11 lost their sight after the age of 5, and 6 suffered from severe vision impairment.

Analyzing the elements of reported NDEs, the researchers conclude that no matter the cause, degree, or length of the visual impairment "the type of NDE reported appears to be much the same and is not structurally different from those described by sighted persons."

Most intriguing is the fact that of the congenitally blind (that is, those blind since birth), almost two-thirds reported <u>being able to see during their experience</u>. Here's how a few of them described their experience:[15]

---

[15] Ring, *Mindsight: Near-Death and Out-of-Body Experiences in the Blind.*

Helen, re two OBEs — reports that in both cases she was able to see her body below. She tells of being excited to see trees and people walking around outside. She also recognized certain friends and various shops in the neighborhood.

Brad, re an NDE as an 8-year-old who stopped breathing and almost died from pneumonia — says he found himself floating near the ceiling of his room at the Boston Center for Blind Children. He saw his roommate get up from his bed and go to get help and he noticed his roommate's "sheets piled partly on the floor and partly on the foot of the bed." Then he went up through the ceiling and the roof of the building and discovered that he could see his surroundings quite clearly. He remembers it being a dark and cloudy day with snow covering everything except, he says, where "the streets themselves had been plowed and you could see the banks on both sides of the streets." He saw the playgrounds beside his building and a trolley passing by.

Cheryl, re an OBE she experienced while lying on her back one summer night — says she had "a tumbling sensation" and found herself looking down at her body from a height of "10 or 12 feet in the air." Then, suddenly, she found herself transported to the house of her girlfriend, Irene. From a vantage point in the doorway of the bathroom, Cheryl observed someone kneeling in front of the toilet. It was another friend, Pat, who was holding her hair back with her left hand as she vomited into the toilet bowl. Cheryl noted the placement of all the ususal fixtures around the bathroom. Later, Pat confirmed (to the researchers) that she and Irene had been partying and "had a few too many to drink, and I ended up getting sick." Pat also confirmed Cheryl's observations that she had been holding her long hair back with her left hand "and everything like that."

Joyce, re one of her OBEs in which she found herself in a flower garden — claims she "saw the colors" of the flowers. She could tell that the air was very warm in the garden and she could hear birds singing, but "the flowers were the most vivid thing." "I can remember all these flowers," she says, even though she admits that she has never seen colors in her physical life.

Vicki, re an NDE after receiving life-threatening injuries in an automobile accident — says she found herself in a non-physical body that was "like it was made of light" viewing the accident scene from above. Then she remembers seeing herself on a table at the hospital and wondering if she was dead. Next, according to the researchers' report of her interview, "she found herself going up through the ceilings of the hospital until she was above the roof," whereupon she saw "a panoramic view of her surroundings" that included "lights and the streets down below." Then she undergoes the tunnel experience and ends up in a place with trees and flowers and people who, in her words "were made of light, and I was made of light." Prior to this Vicki says, she could detect neither light nor shadow and had "never been able to understand even the concept of light."

When an interviewer asked Vicki how she felt about suddenly being able to see, she exclaimed: "I was shocked. I was totally in awe. I mean, I can't even describe it because I thought, 'So that's what it's like!' But then I thought, 'Well, its even better than I could have imagined.'"

End Case 7

Apparently I had a frown on my face when I closed the book.

"Is something wrong?"

"No, nothing's wrong. These are astounding cases. I'm duly impressed. ... I just can't quite wrap my mind around *why* they are so impressive.

"I mean," I paused and thought harder, "I mean, why should it be a big deal that the blind can see during OBEs?

"Being blind," I continued, "is a condition of a person's physical body — their eyes and their nervous system — and no one takes their physical eyes along when they're having an other-body experience. The Seattle Shoe case, for example, would be no more evidential or convincing if Maria had been blind."

"You are exceptionally perceptive and logical," he said.

I beamed.

"Actually, it would have been *less* convincing if Maria had been blind, and thus unable to identify the shoe after Clark retrieved it.

"The cases of blind persons seeing during OBEs and NDEs do not, in fact, add much to the already strong cases, but <u>they greatly strengthen the otherwise contestable ones</u>. Would you care to expand on that?" He looked at me questioningly.

I said nothing, and I stopped beaming.

He said: "I'll give you a hint. Think about dreams."

After a moment, I asked: "Do the blind see in their dreams?"

"As far as I have been able to determine, those persons who have been blind since birth report no sensations in their dreams that they do not have in daily life."

"So, if they don't see in their dreams, but they do see in their OBEs, then there must be something that occurs in an OBE that gives them information that they do not otherwise have.

"When I look at a chair," I continued, motioning toward the recliner he occupied, "I see a chair only because I have learned what sort of visual information can be translated as 'chair.' And I only learned that by having seen lots of chairs from various angles and perspectives."

"That," he said, "is called an experiential referent."

"But, according to these stories, people are seeing flowers and streetlights and toilets and such without any referents possibly existing in their brains."

"Perhaps it's not really 'seeing'," he suggested. "Could it be more of a mental 'knowing' or transcendental awareness?"

I thought long and hard before replying: "Well, it isn't *physical* seeing, but it is perception of light from a distance. I mean, they don't have to touch something to see it and they can't see in the dark, right?"

"Apparently. Very much like our worm cam. But, some OBErs do report being able to see in all directions at once."

"Okay, but that's just a question of seeing at a wider angle than the physical eye is capable of. The 'astral eye,' like the mouth of the wormhole, is localized in time and space; this is not my sense of transcendental awareness.

"For example, when Brad was floating above his roommate's bed in the dorm room, he may have been able to see in all directions at once, but his vision was limited by physical objects and structures, just as physical vision is limited. He saw the sheets piled half on the bed precisely because his view was from that side and because the sheets partially masked his view of the bed and the floor. Again, he did not see the building's surroundings while he was still in the room; he had to travel through the ceilings and reach the outdoors first.

"Or, consider Cheryl in the bathroom doorway or Helen exploring her neighborhood," I continued, warming to my subject, "they don't *just know* what is happening, they observe their surroundings from a particular viewpoint, and if they want a change of scene, they have to move that viewpoint.

"Then there is the matter of scale. Those who report other-body experiences may speak of tiny things such as dust particles on the top of light fixtures, but they see those particles from the same distance as a physical human would. They do not observe the dust particles on the same scale as a dust mite would. Likewise, they observe buildings as large things far away, not as doll houses. If there is no actual astral body, then how are size and scale comparisons made?

"Also, to get back to the light (no pun intended), could one be transcendentally aware of a winter's day being 'dark'? Since darkness is the absence of the sensation of light, would this require being transcendentally aware of a non-awareness?"

"I'm sure I don't know," he said. "A lot of terms have been thrown around in an attempt to explain or rationalize these phenomena, but calling the unknown 'transcendental awareness' or 'extrasomatic vision' tells us no more than it does to claim that we are all part of the Mind of God."

"So, we're stuck with these facts," I summarized. "Blind people observe their OBE environments from the same perspective, viewpoints, scale, and sensitivities as normal vision yet their brains have not been programmed with experiential referents that could help them decipher what they are looking at. These referents must exist in a non-physical mind that is accessible by the non-physical or astral body. And the referents must have been acquired by the mind *prior* to the blind person's physical birth. At least that is the only explanation I can think of at the moment. If I'm right, then OBEs in the blind indicate the existence of a soul prior to birth, and are thus strong evidence for the survival of that soul after death.

"Whatever the case may be, we know that the blind are not dreaming or imagining these visual experiences, and, therefore, we can conclude with some confidence that sighted people are not dreaming or imagining their OBEs either."

"I couldn't put it much better than that," he said with a grin. "Although I might add that the ability of the congenitally blind to see during OBEs might be dependent not just on the preexistence of the soul but on how many physical bodies the soul has lived in prior to this incarnation."

"You mean that the more times a soul had lived, the more experiential referents it might carry with it. That would mean that those souls that don't have visual sensations during OBEs are likely newly born souls."

"Or at least new to Earth," he said, standing up. Why don't you read the next case while I fix us some lunch."

Case 8 – An Out-of-Bed Experience

One sunny afternoon in September, 1958, Robert Monroe tried again to prove that he wasn't crazy. For several months, he had been having what most psychiatrists would call hallucinations or, at least, very weird dreams, in which he seemed to be traveling about the countryside while his body lay inert on his couch at home.

It had all started that Spring. First, without any discernable cause, came hard cramps across his abdomen. Then the shaking started. Or, at least, he felt as if his body was shaking all over, but there was no visible movement. Fearing every nasty affliction from epilepsy to a brain tumor, Monroe fled to his family doctor, but extensive tests revealed nothing out of the ordinary. Soon, a pattern of symptoms developed: several times a week, just as he was nearing sleep, waves of vibrations would sweep over Monroe's body. Then, one night, it happened — he found himself bumping gently along his bedroom ceiling.

Fearing now for his sanity, Monroe sought the advice of a psychologist friend, Dr. Bradshaw. Fortunately for us, instead of sending him off to enjoy a padded cell (where, no doubt, many of his fellow astral travelers are ensconced) Dr. Bradshaw suggested that Monroe ought to stop fighting the sensations and see where they took him.

Where they took him is the subject of three books and the instigation for the founding of the Monroe

Institute.[16] Within a few years, Robert Monroe, once a practical and successful broadcasting executive, became the West's most well-known and influential guru of out-of-body travel.

On the September afternoon in question, Monroe was still trying to confirm that he wasn't simply dreaming his ethereal jaunts. He decided that he would try to leave his body and visit Dr. Bradshaw, whom he knew to be sick in bed. Monroe figured that if he could describe Bradshaw's bedroom, which he had never visited, it would be solid evidence that he was actually out of his body — rather than out of his mind. So, after he achieved lift-out, he focused on Dr. Bradshaw and soon found himself approaching two persons who were walking towards a small out-building of some sort. He was surprised to see that one of the persons was Dr. Bradshaw, dressed not in pajamas, as expected, but in a light-colored overcoat and hat. The other person was Mrs. Bradshaw, dressed in a dark coat and hat. Confused to be observing a scene contrary to the 'reality' he anticipated, Monroe retreated the five miles to his body.

Monroe reported the incident to his wife, who insisted that his observations must be wrong, as she knew that Dr. Bradshaw was ill and in bed that day. That evening, Monroe and his wife telephoned Dr. and Mrs. Bradshaw and asked them where they were between four

---

[16] The books are: *Journeys Out of the Body*, 1971, *Far Journeys*, 1985, and *Ultimate Journey* 1996. The Monroe Institute of Applied Sciences is located in Faber, Virginia, USA. Its website is http://www.monroeinstitute.org.

and five that afternoon. Mrs. Bradshaw stated "that roughly at 4:25 they were walking out of the house toward the garage. She was going to the post office, and Dr. Bradshaw had decided that some fresh air might help him, and he had dressed and gone along."[17] Further questioning revealed that the outer clothing they were wearing precisely matched what Monroe had observed.

End Case 8

I put down the book and carried my iced tea to the table. "One thing that surprises me about these stories is their lack of religious overtones. Don't many folks claim to talk with Jesus during their OBEs, at least the Christians?"

"Many NDErs recall encountering an intelligent and compassionate being. A few take this being to be Jesus or Buddha or whatever figure is consistent with their religious upbringing," he replied. "Sometimes their descriptions change along with those beliefs. I recall one case in which a woman referred to the beings she met as 'spirit people' when she first recounted her experience; but six months later, after she had joined a church, she started referring to them as 'Jesus and the angels.'"[18]

"Most do not make any such identification," he continued, placing a bowl of green grapes on the

---

[17] Monroe, *Journeys Out of the Body*, pp.46-47.

[18] Cox-Chapman, p. 17.

table. "I think it interesting that NDEs are just as likely to happen to those with little or no religious orientation as to those who claim to be very religious.[19]

"Let's eat."

---

[19] Gallup, p. 8.

Morality and the NDA

I wish I did not have to be so grumpy and hard to deal with when I am sick. I positively, almost angrily, dislike being sick. Dying? Dying is another matter. I almost did it once before and found it one of the great, memorable, ecstatic experiences of my life. I can see no reason why the real thing should be less joyous than the trial run.

— Arthur Ford, *The Life Beyond Death,* p. 158.

Breakfast had been a most informal affair of standing around the kitchen sipping coffee and munching on bagels, so lunch was our first meal together. He bowed his head, I followed his lead, and he prayed:

> "As we relax our bodies and prepare them to receive this nourishing meal, we are thankful for our many blessings in this wonderful world. Amen."

"I see you're not a vegetarian," I commented, as I picked up the BLT from my plate and started eating.

"I trust you're not either," he said. "You didn't mention anything about that."

"No. I've never found the discipline to decline a good steak, I'm afraid."

"I don't think that's anything to be afraid of," he responded. "Of course, we all feel better when we eat foods that are good for us, but to avoid certain foods on religious or moral grounds strikes me as rather insulting to the One who created them."

"How so?" I asked, "And, by the way, the sandwich is excellent!"

"That's because the tomatoes are really good this time of year. Now," he looked up and pointed a pickle spear at me, "if *I* were mandating the world's dietary regulations, beef and pork would be fine, but terrible punishments would be inflicted on anyone with taste so poor as to serve those pinkish plastic-like things that pass for tomatoes so much of the year.

"As for the morality of diets," he continued, nibbling on his pointer, "the process of living always involves destruction and rebuilding. That's true of everything from bacteria to beets to Bengal tigers; it's simply the way the physical universe was designed. Perhaps it could have been designed better, but I don't feel qualified to make a judgement on that. Besides, the main point of our discussions this weekend is, in fact, that death is a wondrous transition to a new life."

"For cows and pigs?" I mumbled through a mouthful of bacon.

"To the extent that they possess self-consciousness, I would say so, although I can't say for sure. What I do know is that most of the reports we have from the other side seem to agree with Jesus' statement that the important thing is what comes out of your mouth, not what goes in."[20]

"Perhaps you're right about that," I said, "but didn't God specifically command 'Thou shalt not kill'?"

"Ah! But exactly *who* should not be killed? If you look closely at the history of the Hebrews, as they wrote it themselves in the Torah,[21] you will find that their God clearly had no problem with killing animals — He loved those burnt offerings — or humans. Not only did Jehovah repeatedly encourage the slaughter of various non-Hebrew tribes,[22] but on the first Passover, He took it upon Himself to kill the eldest child in every Egyptian family.[23] Also, other laws of the Hebrew people mandated the death penalty for an amazing number of misdemeanors, including refusing to obey one's parents, picking up twigs on the Sabbath, and using with-

---

[20] See Matthew 15:11 and Romans 14:14.

[21] The first five books of the Old Testament.

[22] Numbers 31 gives one of many gruesome accounts.

[23] Exodus 11:4. For other tales of this death-dealing god, see 2 Kings 19:32-35 and 2 Chronicles 20:14-24

drawal as a form of birth control.[24] Altogether, then, I don't think one can grant much moral authority to the writings of the ancient Hebrews. But, even if you do, there is nothing in the Bible that encourages vegetarianism."

"Yes, I know those gruesome facts well" I said, "You might have added that talking to dead people was likewise a capital crime.[25] But Biblical issues aside, what are your views on the morality of killing?"

"One needs to remember that dying is a necessary part of life; without it our planet would have been overrun with creatures long ago. Have you seen the number of deer in these hills?"

"Driving up here I almost hit several," I answered. "The ones we saw last evening and then there were more walking by when I stepped outside this morning — seems like quite a few; but I'm just a city boy."

"Well, I don't happen to be a hunter," he said, "but it's clear to me that if deer-hunting season weren't so popular up here, the deer population would get out of hand quickly, bringing starvation, pestilence, and more death for all creatures.

"That, of course, is our biggest problem as humans."

"No hunting season on us?" I asked, not certain if he was jesting or not.

---

[24] See Deuteronomy 21:18-21, Numbers 15:32-36, Genesis 38:9.

[25] See Lev 20:27 and Deuteronomy 18:10.

"All our predators have been neutralized except for disease and disasters. We're overrunning the world, yet we're still shocked when epidemics and tsunamis wipe out thousands."

No reply came to me, so I continued munching on lunch.

"Anyway," he resumed after awhile, "something so ubiquitous and necessary as killing could hardly be sinful or immoral in and of itself. In my view — and it's a view endorsed by many revealed teachings — it is not so much the act that counts as the motive.

"An edifying story,[26] if you'll allow one more reference to the Bible, takes place when David was encamped at Ziklag with his exiled band of outlaws and misfits. A man in filthy, torn clothing staggers in to camp, falls to his knees in deference to David, and says that he (the messenger is never named) had been fighting alongside the Israelites when he came upon their king, Saul, wounded and in peril of being captured by the Philistines. Saul calls out to the man in his pain and says 'slay me, for anguish has seized me, and yet my life still lingers.' Seeing that Saul will not live much longer anyway, the man complies with the king's orders, thus saving Saul from a more painful and shameful death at the hands of his enemies. The man then escapes through enemy lines to bring the news of Israel's defeat. He also brings the king's crown, which he believes should now belong to David.

---

[26] As told in 2 Samuel 1:9. See also 2 Samuel 4:10.

"Personally, I believe the man did the right thing in assisting his king to die. David apparently felt differently, he had the messenger executed … although he did keep the crown."

"Wow, I think I need a little time to digest all this," I said, "both the meal and our conversation."

"Then let's take a leisurely stroll in the woods," he suggested and I readily agreed.

The air was warm and fresh and the sunlight dappled the ground as we stepped off the wooden porch and commenced our walk with Dasher prancing at our heels. For awhile, we walked in silence enjoying the sights and sounds of nature. Then he turned towards me and spoke:

"An area the casebook doesn't cover but we ought to at least mention is the NDA."

"Ahh, the NDA," I echoed, as I followed him down a narrow path between tall trees, "standing, I suppose, for Near Death Activities? No, I know, Non-Denominational Allegories?"

"Perhaps you should reconsider vegetarianism," he retorted, using his walking stick to clear away a strand of spider's silk from the path, "the bacon seems to have affected your mind.

"Actually, you're not far off. NDA stands for Nearing Death Awareness. It seems to have been coined to replace the term 'deathbed vision,' probably to encompass other sense impressions such as hearing and smell, and because 'visions' are too closely associated with hallucinations."

"And NDAs are not?"

"As with NDEs, many could be, but the fact that some have imparted information otherwise unavailable leaves us with little choice than to accept them at face value. The literature is full of cases wherein a dying person claims that several deceased friends and relatives are gathering round to aid in their transition to the other side. Any nurse who has worked for long in an intensive-care unit can tell you similar stories. Occasionally, the dying person learns of the death of a loved one by seeing that person among the group."[27]

"Let me get this straight," I said, as we stepped over a leaf-filled culvert and up onto a gravel roadway. "Someone is nearing death, and over a period of ... what, hours, days, weeks?"

"Usually several days."

"Okay, over a period of several days, this dying person reports seeing dead people whom he has known. Are these vivid, realistic images or the more wispy, translucent type of spirits?"

"Real enough so that the dying person often expresses surprise that others cannot see them," he said, picking up a stick from the road and throwing it for Dasher to fetch.

---

[27] For a thorough treatment of this topic, read Osis.

"But how could one set of eyes perceive what another set of eyes cannot?" I wondered.

"Perhaps," he said, "the dying person is beginning to use the same visual apparatus that NDErs use."

"His astral eyes?"

"Good a name as any. Sounds like a song title, doesn't it?" And then he broke into the ardent and rhapsodic palaver of a 1930's radio announcer: "And now, direct from the grand ballroom high atop the NDA building in beautiful downtown Nirvana, Wisconsin, radio KPSI is proud to bring you the otherworldly sounds of Bony Goodman and his spectral orchestra playing that perennial favorite *Astral Eyes*." And, with only the hint of a smile, he turned down another path away from the road.

"You're right," I called to his receding back. "No more bacon for either of us!"

Catching up, I tried to get back on track: "So then, sometimes the dying person sees someone among their ghostly visitors who, as far as the perceiver is concerned, shouldn't be there because that person isn't dead. And they wonder aloud about this in the presence of a nurse or one of their 'real' visitors. And when the matter is investigated, it is discovered that the questionable visitor really has died."

"Or, that the living relatives have known of the death all along but refrained from informing the dying person for fear of unnecessarily upsetting him or her," he added.

"So who coined the term 'NDA'?"

"I believe it was devised by a couple of hospice nurses who wrote a book called *Final Gifts*.[28] I haven't read it myself, but I looked it up a few months ago on the Internet and was astounded to see that 61 out of 62 reviewers gave it 5 stars, the highest possible rating. This is unheard of."

The question hung in the summer air for at least a minute before I broke down. "Okay, I give up, how many stars did the 62nd reviewer give the book?"

"One."

"One," I echoed. "Isn't it wonderful how people can hold such divergent opinions."

"Oh, that reviewer agreed that the book was superb," he said. "He just couldn't accept NDAs because they conflicted with his belief that his church, and his church alone, held the key to heaven's gate."

"Well," I said, ducking under a low branch while stooping to sarcasm, "we certainly can't have those nasty old facts interfering with our beliefs, can we?" But he said nothing and neither did the dog, so I continued: "Are NDAs common?"

"Probably more common than NDEs," he replied, "but it's tough to say. The advent of modern medical care has had a big impact on the reports of NDAs."

---

[28] Callanan.

"Positive or negative?"

> "Both, actually. Positive, because hospitals allow researchers to locate and interview witnesses far easier than when most people died at home. Negative, because so many people now die in a drugged stupor and are in no condition to report anything happening to them."

"You mean they die of drug overdoses," I asked.

> "Oh no! I mean that so many doctors today seem to think that their job is to prevent death, and, since that is impossible, they settle on preventing their patients from *experiencing* death by filling their bodies with pain killers. The so-called 'comfortable' death thus becomes death in a chemical haze. Morphine and other such drugs inhibit memory. This is very likely why only a minority of patients remember NDEs and is almost certainly why many do not report NDAs."

I thought this over as we walked in a silence broken only by an occasional bird call and the rustling of squirrels and chipmunks among the groundcover. I watched several squirrels scrambling to hide behind tree trunks as we approached. The smaller, quicker chipmunks were mostly brown blurs as they zipped between rocks and logs. The deer, I assumed, had heard us coming a mile away for I glimpsed no white tails bobbing over the hills.

The sight of the cabin at the end of our path broke my reverie and refocused me on the topic at hand. "It's interesting," I mused as we climbed the front stairs, "that the NDA is so much simpler than the typical NDE, yet it can be even more evidential of Survival."

"Because the spirits involved are truly dead?"

"Yes," I agreed. "Of course it would be even better if more than one dying soul could get the message."

"Then it must be time to continue our studies," he said, as he opened the cabin door and ushered me inside. "The manual is where you left it."

Saturday Afternoon

The Spirits Speak

Sit down before fact like a little child, and be prepared to give up every preconceived notion, follow humbly wherever and to whatever abysses Nature leads or you shall learn nothing.

— T.H. Huxley[29]

Case 9 – Good Ships and Witches

Gary E. Schwartz, Ph.D., has had an undeniably distinguished career. After being graduated from Cornell as a Phi Beta Kappa, he earned his master's degree in clinical psychology and his Ph.D. in personality psychology from Harvard University. He taught at Harvard and at Yale University, where he became professor of psychology and psychiatry, director of the Yale Psychophysiology Center, and co-director of the Yale Behavioral Medicine Clinic. He has published more than 400

[29] Huxley, p. 330.

articles in peer-reviewed journals and presented over 600 scientific papers, and is currently professor of psychology, medicine, neurology, and psychiatry at the University of Arizona.

In the fall of 1997, during a business trip to Irvine, California, Schwartz was introduced by a colleague to Laurie Campbell, who quickly began offering messages from Schwartz' deceased mother, father, father-in-law, and others. Schwartz was impressed with the accuracy and insight of Campbell's "reading." Especially impressive were Campbell's first words to Schwartz' partner, Linda Russek, when, during this initial meeting, he called to share the experience with her. Upon being handed the telephone receiver, Campbell gave Russek a message from her father: "Thank you for the music." Only upon returning home did Schwartz find out that, years before, his partner had set up a pillow speaker and played cassette tapes for her father as he lay dying in a hospital bed.

Schwartz was by no means ready to believe, but he could not imagine any realistic scenario for Campbell obtaining the information she offered or so accurately mimicking people she had never met. The incident inspired him to set up an experiment testing not only Campbell but also Susy Smith, a medium he had met when he moved to Tucson. The results of this experiment were impressive enough to prompt the development of a university-sanctioned research project that is described in Schwartz' book *The Afterlife Experiments*. Five psychic mediums (George Anderson, John Edward, Anne

Gehman, Suzane Northrop, and Laurie Campbell) participated in one or more experiments, beginning in February of 1999 and still going on as I write this. The results of the experiments to date have been most impressive and the book is well worth reading. The following incident is especially evidential.

What the book calls "The Canyon Ranch Experiment"[30] involved three mediums doing readings for each of five sitters. The mediums worked simultaneously in different rooms. The sitters moved from one medium to another and were sequestered in a separate room while waiting for their turns to come up. The mediums were not told who the sitters were and had no way of telling what order they were being presented. During each session, the medium was prevented from seeing the sitter by two sets of doubled sheets suspended "wall-to-wall and floor-to-ceiling." The medium was prevented from obtaining clues from the sitter's voice by the simple expedient of having the sitter remain silent throughout the experiment. In short, there was no opportunity for the medium to identify the sitter or to base any guesses on the sitters age, gender, health, emotional state, or reaction to a question. During the first ten minutes of each sitting, the sitter did not respond to the medium in any way. After this time period, questions would be answered by an experimenter in the room with the sitter calling out to the medium "yes" or "no" according to a nod or head shake by the sitter.

---

[30] Schwartz, pp. 183-89.

During the totally silent period in which a woman named Sabrina Geoffrion was the sitter, John Edward made two references to an elderly woman that the sitter believes was her grandmother. During the yes/no period (hearing only the experimenter's voice, not the sitter's) Edward said he was being shown daisies at a wedding. The sitter later explained that when her mother married, her grandmother had sewn a ring of daisies into her mother's hair. But it was after the session that the really evidential incident happened.

When Sabrina's session was concluded and she had been escorted to the holding room, Edward's next sitter was brought in. This time, however, the "silent" period was far more silent than usual. Several minutes passed, then Edward claimed that the previous sitter's grandmother had not left when her sitting was concluded. Edward could get nothing about the current sitter, but two impressions came through about the previous sitter: One was the title of the TV show *Sabrina, the Teenage Witch*. The second was *On the Good Ship Lollipop*. the signature song of Shirley Temple.[31]

Later Sabrina explained to Schwartz that it wasn't simply a matter of identifying her name. When she was in school and her classmates taunted her by calling her "Sabrina the witch," her grandmother was the one she would run to for comfort. When Schwartz asked if "on the good ship lollipop" meant anything to her, Sabrina broke out in tears. Although popular long before her

---

[31] First sung in the 1934 movie, *Bright Eyes*.

time, the song was very meaningful to her because, as a young girl, she had curly hair and, when she sang and danced, her grandmother would tell her she looked like Shirley Temple. She had actually sung Shirley Temple songs for her grandmother.

End Case 9

"So, what can we glean from this case?" he asked when I looked up. But the question was apparently rhetorical, for he continued: "First, the possibility of fraud is virtually inconceivable. Schwartz' reputation is impeccable and his honesty unchallenged. Each session was videotaped. John Edward was not told the identity of the sitters and, even if he had somehow discovered the names of one or more, he had no way of knowing their order of presentation."

"So he could not have benefitted from any prior research."

"Right. Also, he never saw or heard the sitter."

"So he had no opportunity to obtain the clues required to do a cold reading."

"And, of special note in this case," he added, "the sitter who was actually in the room with Edward during his most evidential output was not the one for whom he was receiving the information."

"Which argues strongly against mind reading as an explanation."

"Yes. Edward actually asked if the scientists were playing a trick on him by having the same person return for another session.[32] Then, in the face of assurances that it was a new sitter, Edward stuck to his claim that the messages were for the previous sitter, knowing that to do so would cause his accuracy for the current sitting to be rated as zero!"

"Do you think his hits could just be a series of lucky guesses or coincidences?" I asked. "To bring up a wedding is not a big risk for a medium, as most everybody has attended one. On the other hand, to mention such an uncommon flower as a daisy (and not roses or some flower more commonly associated with a wedding) is a bit more daring."

"Even less common than daisies at a wedding," he pointed out, "is 'Sabrina.' Most people would be guessing a long time before they thought of that name. But, it's the song that clinches the matter.

"Consider it this way. Imagine that you are serving on a jury in a murder trial. The victim was found slumped beside a piano with a knife wound in his back. On the piano was a vase of daisies with one plucked stem. On the floor, written in the victim's blood and in his handwriting, was the word 'Sabrina.' Lying open atop the piano was the sheet music for *On the Good Ship Lollipop*."

"Okay," I said, "I can see it all now."

---

[32] This lingering of spirits after the sitter leaves has been reported before. See, *Forty Years of Psychic Research*, by Hamlin Garland, p. 210.

"Shortly after the crime, the police apprehended an ex-lover of the victim named Sabrina. When spotted, she was wearing a plucked daisy in her hair."

"It looks pretty bad for Sabrina."

"And as she was being arrested she kept whistling the tune *On the Good Ship Lollipop*.

"What say you, oh wise and fair juror? Could it all be just coincidental?"

"Guilty, beyond any reasonable doubt." I declared.

"Then," he asked, "can we affirm with equal vigor that John Edward was in actual communication with Sabrina's grandmother?"

"Oh, I suppose the source of the information could be her grand*father* impersonating her grandmother, and I cannot prove that it's not a demon from hell trying to lead us astray or an alien from Ork playing cosmic tricks. But, all things considered, I've got to go with the reality of the spirit of the grandmother as the most likely explanation.

"Once again though, I hate to make a judgement on just one case."

"You know what I think? I think you're already convinced, you're just enjoying yourself too much to quit reading the cases."

"Maybe, maybe not," I said as I picked up the manual again.

Case 10 – From Boys To Woman

In the year 1873, a few of the Fellows of Trinity College, Cambridge, in England, became convinced that neither religion nor philosophy nor history nor science were properly addressing the question of Survival. One of the group later wrote that if anything useful could be learned, it would be learned "simply by experiment and observation ... by the application to phenomena within us and around us of precisely the same methods of deliberate, dispassionate, exact inquiry which have built up our actual knowledge of the world which we can touch and see."[33] In hopes of carrying out such research, the group formed the Society for Psychical Research (SPR), an organization that remains active to this day.

From its beginnings, the SPR attracted a remarkably distinguished membership of scientists, psychologists, philosophers, and politicians who, contrary to what you might think, were generally skeptical of psychic phenomena. Many, in fact, joined with the intention of proving that there was no such thing as the paranormal, and their standards were so strict that some called the SPR "a society for the suppression of evidence."[34]

An early member of the SPR, and a founder of it's American equivalent (the ASPR), was Professor William

---

[33] Myers, p. 5.

[34] Ford, *The Life Beyond Death*, 97.

James of Harvard University. Generally considered one of the greatest psychologists of all time, Dr. James also taught physiology and philosophy and is known as the father of American pragmatism. In the autumn of 1885, James' mother-in-law and sister-in-law attended what may have been the first sitting that Mrs. Leonora Piper ever gave to someone outside of her circle of family and friends. Rumors had been circulating around Boston ever since Piper had discovered her mediumistic talents a few years before, but she had been uncomfortable with the notoriety and had spurned outside sitters. Why his in-laws were granted an exception we do not know, but we do know that they were extremely impressed. Dr. James tried to persuade his in-laws that most marvels had earthly explanations, but he finally gave in to their insistence that he go and see for himself.

A few days later, James and his wife attended a sitting with Piper. So impressed was James that he personally took control of séance arrangements for the ensuing year and a half. Thus began the greatest — longest, best researched, most evidential — chapter in the history of Survival research. First Dr. James, then Professor Richard Hodgson, then Professor James Hyslop investigated and tested Piper over a period of almost 30 years. They brought hundreds of sitters to her under false names. They hired detectives to follow her. They even monitored her mail. They took her to England where she knew no one, kept her in the homes of SPR members, and watched her as closely as any zealous skeptic could wish. In fact, Hodgson, Professor of Legal Studies at

Cambridge University, was known world-wide for his skepticism; he came to America with the announced intention of proving Piper a fraud, as he had done for other supposed mediums. And what, after nearly 16 years of research, did Hodgson conclude? In his own words: "I cannot profess to have any doubt but that the 'chief communicators' to whom I have referred in the foregoing pages, are veritably the personalities that they claim to be; that <u>they have survived the change we call death</u>, and that they have directly communicated with us whom we call living through Mrs. Piper's entranced organism."[35]

To eliminate the possibility of a medium gaining evidential material via telepathy, researchers have often tried asking for facts that are not known to anyone present at the reading. A good example of this, and of Piper's work in general, is the case of Uncle Jerry's Watch.

When Piper was first brought to England she stayed with various members of the SPR. One of her hosts (and investigators) was Sir Oliver Lodge, a professor of physics and mathematics in England and a Fellow of the Royal Society. (Like many others, Lodge was quite skeptical of an afterlife until he had studied Piper. Unlike some others, when faced with the overwhelming evidence Piper and others provided, Lodge possessed the strength of character to admit that he had been wrong and to publicly endorse personal immortality.)

---

[35] Hodgson, Emphasis added.

According to Lodge, in late 1889, he devised an experiment to see if Piper could obtain "<u>facts which were not only out of my knowledge but which never could have been in it</u>."[36]

Lodge had several uncles, at least two of whom were still living, although very elderly, at the time of this test. One of these uncles, whose name was Robert, had been very close to his twin brother, Jerry, who had died some 20 years earlier. Oliver wrote to Robert asking for some object that had belonged to his twin, and Robert responded by sending a gold watch that Jerry had been fond of. Lodge told no one of the watch and, within a few hours of its receipt, he handed it to the entranced Piper.

"I was told almost immediately," Lodge reports, "that it had belonged to one of my uncles ... one that had been very fond of Uncle Robert ... [and] that the watch was now in possession of this same Uncle Robert, with whom its late owner was anxious to communicate. After some difficulty and many wrong attempts, *Phinuit* [Piper's control; the name is pronounced fin-WEE] caught the name, Jerry, short for Jeremiah." Then Lodge heard "This is my watch, and Robert is my brother, and I am here. Uncle Jerry. My watch."

---

[36] This account was originally reported in "A Record of Observations of Certain Phenomena of Trance" by F.W.H. Myers, O. Lodge, W. Leaf, and W. James in *The Proceedings of the Society for Psychical Research*, 1889-90, Vol. 6, pp. 436-659.

Lodge then asked if Jerry could recall trivial details of his boyhood life with Robert. Uncle Jerry "recalled episodes such as swimming the creek when they were boys together, and running some risk of getting drowned; killing a cat in Smith's field; the possession of a small rifle, and of a long peculiar skin, like a snake-skin, which he thought was now in the possession of Uncle Robert." Lodge states that, "these details of boyhood, two-thirds of a century ago, were utterly and entirely out of my ken. My father himself had only known these brothers as men."

And how many of these details could Uncle Robert confirm? According to Lodge: "He recollected something about swimming the creek, though he himself had merely looked on. He had a distinct recollection of having had the snake skin, and of the box in which it was kept, though he did not know where it was then. But he altogether denied killing the cat, and could not recall Smith's field."

Skeptics might well point out that swimming in a creek and playing with a snake skin were hardly unusual activities for boys of that place and age. But in this case, it's the miss that makes the case. For Robert had another brother, name of Frank, an old sea captain living in Cornwall. And Robert, who realized that his memory was failing him, wrote to Frank. And Frank wrote back to say that, indeed, Smith's field was a place where they used to play near their home, in Barking, Essex; and that another of their brothers did kill a cat there. Moreover,

Frank clearly recalled a "foolhardy episode" involving Jerry and him swimming in the creek, near a mill-race.

It should also be noted that, even though Lodge was keeping a close eye on Piper and was confident that she had not hired anyone to snoop out any of the information, he went the extra mile in this case, sending an agent to his uncles' boyhood home to see if the facts given were known by any of the village elders, but the agent could learn nothing.

End Case 10

"This case hardly conforms to my image of a 19th century séance." I said. "You know, a half-dozen gullible folks grasping hands around a table in a darkened parlor while misty ectoplasm swirls among them and whispers issue from a trumpet floating over their heads."

"Yes, such scenes were common at one time, and still occur today at some of the spiritualist enclaves. But Piper, and many other reputable mediums, did not require darkness and did not produce physical effects."

"Did she utilize a trumpet? What the heck is a 'trumpet' anyway?"

"Simply a cone of metal or paper similar to the megaphones used by cheerleaders to amplify their voices. Researchers are justifiably suspicious of those that float around darkened rooms, as many have been proven fraudulent. On the other hand, some mediums — I believe case 16 gives an example — have made honorable use of them under well-lighted test conditions.

"Leonora Piper simply sat down in a chair wherever she was taken and went into a trance. There can be no doubt that her trances were genuine, as she never reacted when she was tested by pricking, cutting, and blistering her skin or by having an open bottle of ammonia held beneath her nose.[37] She spoke in the normal human way. The tone, depth, and inflection of her voice varied with the personalties of those she was channeling, but the only thing spooky about the sittings were the spooks themselves."

"I didn't realize that trances could be so perilous."

"Mediums risk more than you might think. I am reminded of a story Ruth Montgomery tells of a session with the entranced Arthur Ford.[38] At one point, Ford's control, Fletcher, informed Montgomery that the medium was in great pain. Ford 'looked as peaceful as a slumbering child' to Montgomery, but she asked Fletcher to wake him. Immediately upon coming to consciousness, she reports, Ford 'clutched at his heart and groaned in agony.' She knew that he couldn't be faking, Montgomery says, 'for beads of perspiration popped out on his forehead and his suppressed moans tore at my heart.'"

---

[37] Gauld, p. 33.

[38] Montgomery, *A Search for the Truth*, pp. 102-103.

"I'm surprised that Ford's control didn't wake him straightaway the moment the angina began."

"Not only did Fletcher fail to do so; but, after announcing the problem, he actually started to introduce one of Montgomery's deceased relatives! She had to interrupt Fletcher to get him to awaken Ford.

"Such nonchalance is not uncommon for spirit controls. As for Mrs. Piper, I can't say what Phinuit thought of being cut and burned."

"Was Piper able to recall what happened while she was in trance?" I wondered.

"No."

"That must be pretty tough. I mean, we all lose about a third of our lives to sleep, but to give, what?, several hours a day for 30 years just so other people could use you as a telephone. That's a sacrifice few would be willing to make."

"We do owe quite a debt to Piper and those like her," he agreed.

"Were there many others?"

"Piper was special, but she wasn't unique," he said. "It seems that every generation produces a handful of exceptionally talented psychics."

"I wonder why they aren't better known."

"With the possible exception of a few doddering professors of history, we all are inclined to think of the past as impoverished," he said. "A lack of televisions and computers is assumed to mean a corresponding lack of sophistication, knowledge, and even intelligence. Now that the 21st century has dawned, it is even easier to look back with disdain upon those simple bumpkins of the 19th century who actually survived without corn flakes and instant coffee.

"This is a shame," he continued, "because the era that gave us Sherlock Holmes also produced some of the sharpest minds ever to devote themselves to psychical research. The fact that events occurred before we were born, in no way reduces their evidential quality."

"Speaking of the evidence," I said, "the case of Uncle Jerry's Watch is pretty powerful stuff."

"Yes, I believe that the medium and her attending spirit made numerous evidential statements that were later verified." [Together we worked up the following list.]

1. That the watch originally belonged to one of Oliver Lodge's uncles, now deceased.

2. That this deceased uncle's name was Jerry (short for Jeremiah).

3. That the watch was currently owned by another uncle.

4. That the watch owner's name was Robert.

5. That Jerry was very fond of Robert.

6. That when the brothers were young, someone almost drowned while swimming in a creek.

7. That one of the brothers had a snake skin that was kept in a box.

8. That the brothers played in a place called "Smith's field."

9. That one of the brothers killed a cat in that field.

"Now let's see," I said, "Oliver Lodge did not know or have any way of guessing facts 6 through 9, and Uncle Robert could not recall facts 8 and 9 and only vaguely recollected number 6."

"And Uncle Frank," he added, "knew nothing of Jerry's watch and could not remember fact number 7."

"The only one who knew all of the details, then, was the person who provided them in the first place," I pointed out. "And he was dead."

"Therefore," he concluded, "those who believe that all mediumship boils down to mind reading and play acting are left with affirming that Piper somehow read the minds of, and selected specific memories from, not one, not two, but three different people, following some astral trail across England from Oliver's mind to Robert's and thence to Frank's."

"Surely not even our überskeptics would go that far," I avowed.

"Of course not. They deny that minds can be read at all, and for good reason. I think a fellow named Whately Carington said it most succinctly: 'Survival is a spectacular issue, but not a crucial issue; it is telepathy that is crucial though it may not be spectacular.'[39]"

"Meaning, I suppose, that the existence of telepathy proves that a non-physical reality exists, thus establishing an environment for the continuance of the discarnate soul."

"Yes, but it's more than that. You know, it isn't so difficult to accept that we can mentally send and receive thoughts; the tough part is figuring out how a mind could sort through all the billions of thoughts that are being sent out at any given moment and read only the sought for message."

"Yes, I can see that the problem is not in the transmission or the reception but in the tuning."

"Without some structure, all any mind could ever receive is the 'white noise' created by the intermingling of the thoughts of every being in the universe. And this argues strongly for the existence of some sort of universal mind or discarnate communications system that routes and delivers mental images according to our intention or desire. Such a system couldn't be limited to our own minds; it would have to exist in a mental plane independent of the physical."

"I'm not sure I follow," I said. "The TV tuner that separates the signals is a part of the television set. Why

---

[39] Carington, p. 3.

couldn't our brains contain the 'telepathy tuner' necessary to sort through the waves of thoughts?"

"The television tuner works because it was calibrated at the factory to match up with signals of specific wavelength agreed upon by the broadcasters and the manufacturers. This system of agreements is not designed and maintained within the television set. Likewise, the system that allows one person to receive the thoughts of another person cannot be sustained by either party alone or together. It must have an independent, non-physical superstructure."

"Okay, I got that. Wouldn't the same argument apply to instances of clairvoyance or OBEs. I can conceive of an astral body as simply an appurtenance of the physical one, but to travel to a specific place would require an astral map of some sort, a map that could only exist in that same autonomous spiritual plane."

"Precisely. In fact, as Carington concludes: 'The phenomena of telepathy, etc., are therefore not an alternative to survival, but a virtual guarantee of it.' Which is why the überskeptics refuse to admit to ESP despite decades of solid proof of its existence.

"No, the only people who would even suggest mental telepathy as an explanation for Mrs. Piper's success are those parapsychologists who postulate the existence of super-psi."

"And what, pray tell, is super-psi?"

"Super-psi, or super-ESP, is the nebulous notion that anything a discarnate spirit might do could also be accomplished by some extreme (and usually speculative) power of a living mind. That is, that some combination of telepathy, clairvoyance, precognition, and/or mind-control is in play rather than actual communication with the dead."[40]

"Where does mind-control come into it," I wondered.

"Many places, but the most salient would be the Cross-Correspondences."

"I've heard something of those, but I'm not real clear on how they worked," I admitted.

"At one time, a few discarnate spirits had the idea that they could provide unchallengeable proof of the continued survival of their personalities by sending different parts of a message to different sitters via different mediums," he explained. "Each piece of this puzzle was designed by the spirits to make little or no sense by itself, but when the various pieces were read within the context of the others, a clear message would be seen."

"And these spirits actually accomplished this?"

"Beginning in 1901, several mediums associated with the SPR (Piper among them) who were spread across England, the United States, and India, began producing such messages. These cross-correspondences flowed freely for over three decades, ultimately comprising more than 3,000 scripts taking up some 12,000 typewritten sheets. The results were very impressive."

---

[40] See, for example, Braude.

"Then why aren't they better known?"

"Two reasons, I think," he replied. "For one, they are too complex for their own good. The very aspects that make them so evidential also make them difficult to comprehend. Of course, it doesn't help that the spirit who initiated the whole program was a classical scholar; many of the references are obscure passages in Latin and Greek."[41]

"Ouch! I can see the first problem. Does the second involve super-psi?"

"How did you guess?

"Must be psychic," I shrugged. "So, despite the spirits' long and convoluted efforts, some folks still insist that they don't exist and that these correspondences were caused by mental powers of the living?"

"Correct. For some reason, they evidently feel an overwhelming urge to deny the possibility of an afterlife, and when the evidence is objectively evaluated, super-psi is the only alternative they have.

"To get back to our point, do you see the problem with several mediums who are spread across the globe simultaneously constructing a puzzle of Latin and Greek phrases that none of them understand?"

---

[41] Those interested in delving deeper should consult some of the many analytical pieces available. (More than 50 papers, many of them book-length, have been written by SPR members alone.)

"Well," I pondered a moment. "I reckon there has to be some central cause of it all."

"Exactly. The only explanation for this, besides Survival, is that one of the sitters must be using his super powers to broadcast the messages into the mediums' subconscious minds while causing them to hallucinate their contacts on the other side."

"But that's ridiculous!" I exclaimed.

"More than ridiculous," he replied, "absolutely scary! I wonder sometimes if those who support the super-psi notion have considered the implications of someone actually having these awesome powers. If such a one could read one mind, he could read everyone's mind. If such a one could influence one mind, he might, even now, be influencing all of our minds. The existence of super-psi would be the paranoiacs worst nightmare."

I slowly scanned the cabin ceiling and said under my breath: "You wouldn't happen to have any kryptonite around here, would you?"

"I don't believe you have any need to worry," he assured me, "there are a lot of cases that are very difficult if not impossible to explain via super-psi." And he nodded to me to continue reading.

Case 11 – Evidence by the Book

"Book Tests" are a category of evidence in which a discarnate entity directs an incarnate person to words or phrases written in a place never previously accessed by that person, thereby communicating a message that could not be a product of mind reading or unconscious creation by the living. The first book tests on record were initiated in 1917 during sessions held by Gladys Osborne Leonard, one of the most renowned mediums in England.

Once, when the Reverend Drayton Thomas was having a sitting with Leonard, the spirit of his father came through and told him that he had tried to communicate in the past by knocks and raps but had failed to make sufficiently distinctive and noticeable sounds.[42] A few nights later, Thomas was at home when he heard a systematic rapping punctuated three times by a loud double knock.

When next he attended a session with Leonard, the Reverend was told by *Feda* (Leonard's control) that his father had asked her to make the knocks, so she had gone to his house and attempted to spell her name using Morse code. Then *Feda* announced that the elder Thomas had devised a test. The son was to go to the bookshelf behind the door of his study, and from the second shelf up, withdraw the fifth book from the left.

---

[42] Smith, pp. 75-76.

Near the top of page 17, he would find words describing what had occurred.

When Thomas did as instructed, he discovered that the fifth book from the left on the second shelf was a volume of Shakespeare, and in the third line from the top of page 17 (Act I, Scene 3 of King Henry VI) was the phrase: "I will not answer thee with words, but blows."

End Case 11

"I've seen stage magicians that could tell what was written on a particular page and line of a book."

"Yes, and you can buy the trick books they use in most magic shops or online. You may also have seen or read magicians telling how to perform such feats with a person's own books," he continued, "but this always requires a minute or so of private access to the library to set up the trick. Our dear Mrs. Leonard, on the other hand, was not a professional magician and had never set foot in the Thomas home.

"So, Leonard would have had to conceive of the play on words that linked the raps with the Shakespeare quote, then mentally searched the son's library for a book containing *Henry VI Part I*, and then somehow read pages without opening the book."

"The very task we agreed was impossible with neither light, nor lens, nor perspective."

"Yes."

"But," I wondered, "how is that evidence for Survival? I mean, what advantage would a discarnate spirit have that would allow *it* to accomplish such a feat?"

"I don't know," he admitted. "But it was the father's library, so it is more probable that the information came from his memory than from the medium's conjectured (and incomprehensible) ability to read closed books at a distance. And, of course, we have *Feda's* testimony, which we have no ground to discount.

"On the other hand, perhaps the plane that supports astral bodies also has astral books that can be read with astral eyes even when their physical counterparts remain closed and on the shelf.

"Now consider a similar case sans the involvement of a medium."

Case 12 – Jung's Dream Library

The famous psychoanalyst, C.G. (Carl Gustave) Jung tells of a sort of uninvited book test in the form of a vision.[43] One night, as he lay in bed feeling deeply concerned about the recent death of a friend, Dr. Jung sensed that friend's presence in the room. At first, Jung doubted his feelings, but then he decided that proof was irrelevant and that he might as well give his spectral visitor the benefit of the doubt. "The moment I had that thought," Jung relates, "he went to the door and beckoned me to follow him."

[43] Jung, pp. 312-313.

And so, Dr. Jung followed (in his vision) his friend "out of the house, into the garden, out to the road, and finally to his house. ... I went in and he conducted me to his study. He climbed on a stool and showed me the second of five books with red bindings which stood on the second shelf from the top."

Jung was unacquainted with the man's study and did not know what books he owned. Curious, he went the next morning to his friend's widow and obtained permission to "look up something" in the man's library. "Sure enough," he reports, "there was a stool standing under the bookcase I had seen in my vision, and even before I came closer I could see the five books with red bindings. I stepped up on the stool so as to be able to read the titles. ... The title of the second volume read: 'The Legacy of the Dead.'"

End Case 12

"The argument for the Survival explanation is even stronger in this example because there is no third party involved and because the beckoning friend clearly implies a planned destination. On his own, Dr. Jung could have had an OBE and might have envisioned his recently departed friend, but he had no reason to travel to his friend's library. The impetus for that trip could only have come from his friend's spirit."

"And, even if he had dreamed up the library visit," I added, "why would he envision the book but not the book's title?"

"Why, indeed?"

"Was Jung a believer in Survival?"

"Although he never confirmed such a belief in his books, Jung once wrote in a letter that 'In each individual case I must of necessity be sceptical, but in the long run I have to admit that the spirit hypothesis yields better results in practice than any other.'" [44]

Case 13 – Where's the Smoke?

Sometimes, the writing to be discovered is neither in a book nor on its cover. One of the better known examples of this type of phenomena was reported by Thomas Sugrue in his book on the famous psychic, Edgar Cayce. [45]

According to Wesley Ketchum, M.D., who worked with Cayce early on, one of the ingredients in a recommended preparation was specified by the entranced Cayce as "Oil of Smoke." Dr. Ketchum had never heard of Oil of Smoke and the local druggists could find no such item in their catalogs. Ketchum had no alternative but to have another reading in hopes of determining where this arcane substance could be found.

[44] Wilson, p. 131.
[45] Sugrue, p. 25.

Cayce directed them to a drugstore in Louisville, KY (about 150 miles away), but the manager of that drugstore responded to their telegram by saying that he had never heard of Oil of Smoke. Again, a reading was held, and this time very detailed directions were given. A bottle of the substance would be found on a specified shelf in the back of the store, behind a bottle of another preparation (which was named).

This time, the Louisville store manager wired back: "Found it." As Ketchum reported: "The bottle arrived in a few days. It was old. The label was faded. The company which put it up had gone out of business. But it was just what he said it was, 'Oil of Smoke.'"

End Case 13

"I'm surprised Cayce hasn't come up earlier," I said.

"As impressive as some of his work is, little of it makes a strong case for Survival," he replied. "Cayce definitely did some efficacious diagnostic work and many of his prescribed treatments bordered on the miraculous. But then, he was also mistaken on many occasions when he wandered from the medical arena."

"Some writers claim he was wrong all the times that he wasn't just lucky."

"You've been reading the überskeptic's websites again, haven't you? They love to talk in generalities and innuendos. I've even seen a couple that mention the Oil-of-Smoke case, but only to point out that this is just an old name for Beechwood Creo-sote, as if Cayce was trying to mislead folks. As far as I know, the critics have never bothered to mention the astounding way the bottle was located.

"As for being lucky, well, consider one of his first patients, a 5-year-old girl who was diagnosed by medical doctors in Cincinnati as having a rare brain affliction that was invariably fatal.[46] She was having convulsions up to twenty times a day and her mind would appear totally blank. Her parents had brought her home to die, when a family friend suggested that Edgar Cayce might be able to help. And so, for the price of the railroad ticket, Cayce left his job as a bookstore clerk in Bowling Green and came back to Hopkinsville. (At the time, he thought he needed to be near the patient to do a reading.)

"In trance, Cayce said that when the girl was two years of age she had influenza (a fact he had no way of knowing) and that the flu germs had settled in her spine due to an injury she had sustained immediately before. (The girl's mother later testified that no one but herself knew that the girl had slipped getting out of a carriage the day before contracting the flu and had hit the end of her spine on the carriage step.) After undergoing the treatments Cayce recommended, the girl returned to normal, completely healed of her 'fatal' disease.

---

[46] Sugrue, pp. 19-22.

"I don't think either the girl or her mother would admit to any "luck" being involved in that case, and there are scores of others like it in the Cayce files."

"I second your endorsement," I said, "I've always felt that Cayce provided an excellent example of one's beliefs *not* influencing trance pronouncements. In trance, he often spoke of a patient's past lives, although the conscious Cayce resisted the idea of reincarnation as contrary to his Christian faith.

"Nevertheless, I wonder if the detection of the bottle is such good evidence for Survival."

"Do you find it easier to accept the existence of a discarnate intelligence being in contact with a retired pharmacist or that a living person could clairvoyantly search the shelves of every drugstore in Kentucky for a single small bottle."

"That does seem to stretch the concept of super-psi about as much as the case of Uncle Jerry's Watch."

"I think you'll find that the next two cases stretch it beyond the breaking point," he said, motioning once again towards the *Casebook*.

Case 14 – The R101 Disaster

On Saturday the 4th of October 1930, at 6:24 in the evening, the airship R101 slipped its moorings in Cardington, England, and began its maiden voyage to India. Under the command of Flight-Lieutenant H. C. Irwin, the R101 was the largest airship (otherwise known as a dirigible, zeppelin, or blimp) in the world. Its departure had been hurried to avoid stormy weather threatening along its route through France. The R101 was a new design and, like many new designs before and after it, had been pressed into service for political reasons without all the tests and trials that prudent policies might have dictated.

Less than 8 hours later, 46 of the 54 passengers and crew of the R101 were dead[47] and its fire-blackened skeleton loomed over a soggy meadow near the town of Beauvais, just north of Paris. Early on Sunday morning, heavy rains and gusting winds had brought the nose of the behemoth almost gently down to earth, but a rotating propeller on a starboard engine dug into the dirt, causing the engine to twist and ignite the hydrogen gas flowing from rents in the forward gas bags. It only took a moment for the entire ship to be engulfed in flames.

The R101 disaster shocked the British nation. It shook the government's confidence in dirigibles, and ended British efforts to develop lighter-then-air craft for commercial use. Several months were required for investigators to determine all the factors that contributed to the disaster, but a small gathering of private citizens in London knew, only two days after the crash, what the findings would be.

---

[47] Two other crew members later died of injuries sustained in the crash, bringing the total dead to 48.

On Tuesday, the 7th of October, 1930, at 3 p.m., a séance was held at number 13 Roland Gardens in London, home of the National Laboratory of Psychical Research. The laboratory had been founded 5 years before by Harry Price. A keen investigator and talented magician, Price had a reputation for exposing fraudulent mediums. Joining Price for the afternoon séance were Ethel Beenbarn, Price's secretary and stenographer; journalist Ian D. Coster, who had requested the session in the hope of contacting the spirit of Sir Arthur Conan Doyle; and Eileen Garrett, a medium of growing renown in England. This was Garrett's first visit to Price's laboratory; she did not know Coster nor had she been told the purpose of the session.

Garrett went immediately into trance and her control, *Uvani*, began to speak. He spoke not of the recently passed-on Doyle, however, but of a man named "Irwin" who was apologizing for interfering but who insisted on speaking. Then, as Price reports[48] "the voice of the medium again changed and an entity announced that he was Flight-Lieutenant H. Carmichael Irwin, captain of the R101. He was very agitated, and in a long series of spasmodic sentences gave the listeners a detailed and apparently highly technical account of how the R101 crashed."

The reporter, Coster, was at first miffed that he wasn't getting an interview with Doyle, but he quickly realized he was witnessing a historic event. He put the

---

[48] Price, *Leaves from a Psychist's Case-Book*, chapter 6.

story out at once, and newspapers across England and around the world carried it, often with banner headlines. Transcriptions of the session were requested and carefully studied by experts investigating the crash, one of whom asked for and received an additional séance to further interview the R101's deceased crew. The government never officially endorsed Garrett's work, of course, but an official named Charlton, who examined the transcription in great detail claimed that the idea that anyone at the seance could have obtained such technical information beforehand was "grotesquely absurd."

Several of Irwin's statements — such as the ship being too heavy for its engines — were public assumptions or could be reasonably guessed. But many were technical, confidential, or simply unknown to anyone at the time. Here are three examples of such.

Irwin said: "Load too great for long flight. Same with SL-8. Tell Eckener."

No one at the seance knew the meaning of "SL-8" or recognized the name "Eckener." The British experts who reviewed transcripts of the session knew that Dr. Eckener was the designer of the *Graf Zeppelin*, but even they had to search through their records of German airships to discover that "SL-8" was the identifier for a dirigible built by the Schütte-Lanz company of Mannheim, Germany.

Irwin said: "Starboard strakes started."

"Strakes," a term foreign to all at the session, was originally a naval expression that was adopted by airship designers. Strakes are parallel layers of longitudinal plates that form the sides of a ship. Irwin was formerly a navy man, so it is a term that he would be likely to use.

Irwin said: "Impossible to rise. Cannot trim. Almost scraped the roofs of Achy. Kept to railway."

Achy, a French village 12½ miles north of Beauvais, was on the R101's route. Achy was shown on the type of large-scale air-ordnance map carried by the R101, but the village was so small that it did not appear on any normal ordnance or road map. Neither did it rate mentioning in Baedeker's or Michelin's guidebooks. It does lie on the main rail line between Amiens and Beauvais. Witnesses near the town testified that the airship had passed over extremely low.

Harry Price concluded: "It is inconceivable that Mrs. Garrett could have acquired the R101 information through normal channels and the case strongly supports the hypothesis of survival."[49]

End Case 14

"Where were the survivors of the crash when the séance was held?"

"They were still in a French hospital."

"Could Garrett have been reading one or more of their minds?"

---

[49] Price, *Fifty Years of Psychical Research*, p. 153.

"Of the eight crew who survived, five maintained the engines, one operated the radio (wireless), and two were riggers. It is unlikely that they would have had lengthy commentary on the faults in the ship's design, and extremely unlikely that they would have been thinking of Eckener and the SL-8."

"Was the radio operator who survived on duty when the ship crashed?"

"As a matter of fact, he wasn't. He was asleep in his bunk and only awakened when the ship went into a steep dive. Why do you ask?"

"Well, I thought that if the radio operator had been in the control car he might have seen the map and been aware of the name of the village they nearly scraped the roofs from."

"I hadn't thought of that; but, you're right. The most unlikely thing of all is that any of the survivors would have been aware that the ship had just passed over a village named Achy.

"But, of course, nothing can be ruled out 100 percent."

"Well, this case comes very close to being 100 percent convincing."

"The next one comes even closer."

Case 15 – Relics Revealed

In 1914, as Violet Parent was recovering from a severe illness, her deceased mother appeared to her and told her she would find a gold coin above one of the doorways in her apartment. Her husband, Gregory, later reported: "We both considered this merely a dream, for our apartment had just been thoroughly cleaned. Nevertheless, we looked, and sure enough, over a door leading to the porch we found a ten-dollar gold piece."[50]

Now, the Parents were of very modest means. He was a grocery clerk and she a housewife. They lived in a "two-room apartment of threadbare aspect." Thus they were most impressed by such a find, and so, understandably, they paid close attention to Violet's ensuing visions.

Shortly, she began to fall into trances in which other spirits spoke to her. Some of these spirits claimed to be missionaries who had spent much of their earthly lives trying to convert the natives of Mexico, Southern California, and Arizona to Christianity. Other spirits said they had been Indians who were the subjects of these conversion attempts. Mrs. Parent, an illiterate woman who had

---

[50] This coin was just under ¾ inch (1.75 cm.) in diameter. Ten dollars then would equate to about $187 now. (The coin itself would actually be worth several thousand today). How it got above the Parent's door was never discovered.

grown up in St. Louis, had no idea what they were talking about. But, she understood quite well when the spirits directed her to other caches of money buried or hidden here and there around their hometown of Redlands, California. Within 6 years, the Parents had found sufficient funds to purchase their first house and automobile.

The locations of the loot were only revealed to give the Parents the means to pursue the agenda of the missionaries. They told Violet that the natives had buried numerous crosses and other religious artifacts through-out the Southwest. The padres had decided to try and prove their continuing existence in the spirit world by directing people to the location of these crosses. This would be exactly what skeptics had been asking for since the first claim of Survival was made: <u>the spirits would reveal information that no one living knew or could have known</u>.

And reveal it they did, and not just once, or twice, or thrice, which ought to have been proof enough. Over a period of 10 years, the Parents were directed to more than 50 widely separated locations across a region 600-miles long by 300-miles wide. Once they arrived at the location specified they were directed to a particular hillside or streambed or other landmark and told what they should find buried there. Sometimes the search was fruitless; perhaps because someone had already discovered the treasures, perhaps due to heavy rains or earthquakes, or it could be that the Indians simply mis-remembered the location of a ceremony. But the quests were successful often enough to net more than 1,500 crosses and other sacred objects!

Yes, you read that right. Information that only people long dead could possibly know enabled living people to find real, solid, manmade items FIFTEEN HUNDRED times! All this in addition to hundreds of finds of gold, silver, and paper money crammed into tins and bottles, or wrapped in oilskins or decaying leather pouches that had been carefully buried by the denizens of the desert and never retrieved.

At first, the Parents did not own a car, so they had to rely on neighbors and friends to chauffeur their excursions. Typically, Violet would direct the group to the designated site (often hundreds of miles from their home) and then the others would dig in the ground, chop at cactus, or pry up boulders as necessary to reveal and retrieve the crosses. Violet, being somewhat delicate and very fearful of rattlesnakes, did little digging herself. Numerous affidavits exist, signed by people who assisted on one or more of these expeditions, testifying that they found crosses precisely where the spirits predicted.

We know all of this because Gregory Parent kept detailed notes that ultimately filled 22 journals. He gave the dates and times of every excursion and he listed every item in every find. Most importantly for posterity, 5 years after his wife died, he wrote a letter to a man named Hamlin Garland.

Garland was a Pulitzer-prize winning author of over 50 books, mostly novels and biographies. Mr. Parent was likely attracted to him because his most recent book[51] was an account of his personal experiences as an investigator for the American Society for Psychical Research. Garland was intrigued enough by what he read in the letter to visit Parent at his apartment and view his journals and several pictures of the crosses. Parent wanted Garland to write a book about the discovery of the crosses. Garland liked the idea, but being busy with other matters, he did not attempt to contact Parent again for almost 2 years, by which time Parent had died.

It took several months, but Garland managed to track down and obtain the entire collection of crosses along with Gregory Parent's journals and papers. The names of many people who had assisted the Parents in their searches were listed in the papers and Garland was able to locate fifteen of them — all of whom confirmed Parent's reports. As an example, in one interview a woman told Garland: "I myself picked up two containers for her — one from the sand on the seashore and one from the bed of a stream. To say that Violet had 'planted' these gold pieces and these wads of bills is absurd. She never had coins to plant, and furthermore, the rusted and rotted condition of these containers proved their long situation in the ground."

From these interviews and papers, Garland learned enough of the Parent's story to begin work on a book. From that book, appropriately titled *The Mystery of the*

---

[51] Titled *Forty Years of Psychical Research*.

Buried Crosses and published in 1939, the facts and quotes given here are derived.

As for the artifacts themselves, Garland notes that they were stored in "seventeen flat, glass-covered boxes, each case numbered and the places of discovery carefully recorded." No other classification had been done, so Garland sorted them into three groups as follows.

• The first grouping contained 70 figures of Christ about 3 inches long with uplifted arms [presumably from, or intended for, crucifixes]. These were probably made some 200 years earlier in the area of New Spain that would become Mexico and given out to the Indians by the Spanish padres. Garland classified them as "missionary period" along with numerous crosses and small tablets stamped with dates (from 1769 to 1800) and the names of celebrated padres. These vary from 5 to 18 inches in length. According to the spirits, they were fashioned by artisans at the Mission of San Juan Capistrano.

• The second, and far larger, class contained crosses that impressed Garland as "wholly barbaric in character and immensely older" than the first group. The crosses (most single-barred but some double-barred) bore representations of various animals (such as wolves, apes, and birds), fruits, shells, etc. molded upon them. The figures were tribal totems and the crosses were paraphernalia for sun-worship ceremonies imported from Central America, according to the spirits.

• Garland's third category consisted of crosses and plaques that bore human faces. The character of these faces seemed distinctly Oriental rather than Aztec or Spanish. Some of the heads were crowned with turbans and others wore tall headdresses. Perhaps the most amazing aspect was that no two of these artifacts were alike. In fact, Garland noted, this collection "appeared to be the work of many hands and many minds, not to say generations."

Most of the crosses were of varying alloys of lead, tin, copper, antimony, iron, and aluminum. Some were of silver and a few were gold.

End Case 15

"This is huge," I asserted.

"Yes."

"I mean really HUGE!

"Like, why haven't I heard of this before? Why hasn't everybody heard of this?"

"So," he said, "you still have questions."

"Yeah, I've got questions. Where are the crosses now? What motivated the Parents to do all that work? Have others authenticated the crosses? Has anyone else ever found such crosses? Are there any left? There must be some still out there. Do you know any good mediums? I'll bring a metal detector. How soon can we go?

"Whoa back!" he said. "I appreciate your enthusiasm and I'll answer your questions, but first I have a question for you: What difference would it make?"

"What difference would what make?"

"The answers to any of the questions you just asked, or any questions that might be asked. What possible impact could they have on the level of proof for Survival provided by this case?"

I was still pondering this when he spoke up and said: "Let's break down exactly why this case is so evidential. The claim is that something was found that could not possibly have been found without information held only by dead folk. This breaks down into two separate claims. The first is that something was found. How certain can we be of that?"

"Well, if the crosses were not discovered by the Parents, then they were already available to them. Is there any evidence of that?" I asked.

"Not that I've been able to find."

"Then, are there any records of such crosses existing previously?"

"Garland could find only two references to the native crosses — a single footnote in an obscure padre's journal quoting an explorer as saying that in 1604 (150 years before the establishment of the first mission) he had come upon a tribe that wore crosses in their hair,[52] and a picture in the *Handbook of the American Indian*, of a similar cross dug from a

---

[52] Garland, *The Mystery of the Buried Crosses*, p. 165.

mound in Wisconsin.[53] Unknown to Garland, two similar crosses had been found in 1832 at an Indian grave-mound in Georgia and an additional eight crosses were unearthed in 1924 near Tucson Arizona."[54]

"So there is evidence that this kind of thing existed, but no one is known to have possessed a large collection of them."

"That is correct. And," he continued, "that is why the crosses are so much more evidential than the money. As silly as it is to think that Violet Parent went all over Southern California planting gold and silver coins just so she could dig them up again, it is *possible* for her to have done so, because such coins were theoretically within her reach. This remote possibility would weaken the case slightly."

"I see your point," I said. "Violet could not have begged, borrowed, or stolen the crosses because the crosses simply were not available. And, if she didn't have them, she could not have planted them."

"Which is why the large number of artifacts is important to the case. If only three crosses had been recovered, the charge that they had been planted by the Parents might carry some weight, even if all three had been found buried beneath a couple of feet of undisturbed ground (as many were). But 1,500 items negate any such possibility. One might

---

[53] *Ibid*, p.36

[54] Steiger, pp. 41-47.

just as well believe that they were all planted by Paul Bunyan with the magical assistance of Babe the Blue Ox."

"So the first claim has been satisfied," I said, "we are certain that something was found."

"Now we consider if there is or was any way that the crosses could have been found other than by direction of the dearly departed."

I shook my head slowly, "The only half-way reasonable alternative I can think of is maybe God told her."

"I'm generally reticent to guess God's reasons for anything," he said, "but I can't imagine why He would need to pose as dead padres and spread lies about the afterlife."

"Good point. ... Well, there's always the worm cam."

"Or Violet was adept at traveling the desert in her astral body. Only one problem with either of those conjectures: How did she know where to look? Maybe, just maybe, I could accept that Violet's wandering soul somehow happened to stumble upon one of the crosses ... "

"I like the image of a stumbling soul," I grinned.

"But to find them over and over again throughout an area of some 200,000 square miles? Never. ... The most super super-psi imaginable couldn't account for that. No. The only conceivable way anyone could consistently locate all those crosses is to be given directions by the persons who hid them."

"It all adds up to an extraordinarily solid proof of Survival," I said. "The only thing it lacks is replicability. Someone needs to repeat what the Parents did and find more crosses. I suggest we do that now." I stood up and stretched.

"I suggest you keep reading," he said.

I sat down, turned the page, and read.

Case 16 – Relics Revealed Revisited

When Hamlin Garland received the letter from Gregory Parent, he had just published *Forty Years of Psychic Research*, a book he felt was the final summation of his work as an investigator of the paranormal. But the letter, and the journals, papers, and artifacts he subsequently discovered, brought an unexpected and astounding capstone to his avocation. Indeed, what Garland titled "The Mystery of the Buried Crosses" would prove to be one of the most convincing, if not *the* most convincing, arguments for the survival of human consciousness after physical death.

Once he had read Parent's journals and gazed upon the 1,500 crosses with his own eyes, Garland knew that he had been handed a case of supreme importance. He also knew that the case needed to be verified by an independent researcher duplicating the feat of finding such items buried in the California desert. Despite being 76 years old, Garland realized that this task had fallen on his shoulders.

His first step was to find a medium who could contact the spirits of Gregory or Violet Parent or of the missionaries themselves. As he was considering who might be best suited for the job, Garland received a letter from a Dr. Nora Rager in Chicago who had read *Forty Years of Psychical Research* and wished to introduce him to a medium named Sophia Williams, who had recently moved to Los Angeles. Garland interviewed Williams and found her perfect for the job. She was friendly, could work anywhere (indoors or out), anytime (day or night), was anxious to help, and made no charge for her services. As Garland writes: "It was in this providential way that I found myself in possession of a most intelligent co-investigator."[55]

In her very first session, Williams immediately became a conduit for several of Garland's deceased friends. One of whom, Henry Fuller, often acted as a control in the coming sessions. But it wasn't just the obvious acquaintances of Garland who spoke through Williams in that first session; spirits that he hardly remembered showed up, and at least one fellow that he didn't know at all. The latter identified himself as Harry Friedlander, a recently deceased friend of the stenographer whom Garland had hired to take notes of the session. Williams had never met the stenographer nor did she know he would attend the session. Friedlander accurately described his recent death in an airplane accident. Garland refers to this performance by Williams

---

[55] Garland, *The Mystery of the Buried Crosses*, p. 49.

as "our first evidence of her power." There would be a lot more.

At their third sitting, on March 17, 1937, the spirit of Violet Parent spoke through the medium. She affirmed that there were more crosses to be found and she promised the aid of the padres in finding them. As the sessions continued, many of the missionaries did come through, plus several early explorers of the American Southwest.

Besides the veridical material received through Sophia Williams, there came some interesting, and reassuring, insights into the afterlife. One of the padres noted: "We have all changed our opinions about many things — not only about the Indians, but about religion. We learn the truth on this side. ... We have found now that there is no difference in creed."

All that Garland and company managed to get from their first few expeditions were good lessons in how hot the desert could get, how steep the hills, how hard the ground, and how prickly the cactus that seemed to grow everywhere. Then on the 15th of May, 1937, while digging as instructed near the roots of an ancient oak tree some 75 miles northeast of Los Angeles, Garland's daughter, Constance, struck a cross.

Greatly inspired by this first find, Garland et al took every opportunity to make the lengthy excursions pre-scribed by the spirits. The story of the successes and failures of these trips is well told in Garland's book. Suffice it to say here that a total of 16 crosses were discovered in widely scattered and generally difficult-to-reach locations.

And so, the "research" of the Parents was duplicated and authenticated. People with no connection to the Parents, once again, have been able to find something that could not have been consistently found without information held only by the supposedly dead.

End Case 16

"Do you still want to go searching for crosses?"

"It sounds like it would be fun," I replied. "Although, by now, most of the remaining ones are probably entombed in the foundations of condominiums and strip malls."

"So, did your questions get answered?"

"The more I learn, the more I want to know. I intend to read that book and get the full story. But I still want to know where the crosses are now."

"Garland's granddaughter inherited[56] those that he and Williams found and she donated them to the West Salem Historical Society. This organization is housed in the Garland homestead in the town of West Salem in the county of, believe it or not, *La Crosse*, Wisconsin.[57]

---

[56] Garland died within a year after he completed his book on the crosses; he was 79.

[57] So named by French explorers when they saw Winnebago Indians on the prairie playing a game similar to the French game of lacrosse.

"As for the original 1,500 unearthed by the Parents, Garland donated them to a California museum, but no one seems to be sure what happened to them after that. As we speak, a journalist by the name of Michael Tymn[58] is working to unravel this second mystery of the buried crosses."

"So we've got the 16 crosses Garland found, but we have only his word that the 1,500 others ever existed?

"The word of a highly respected man with an impeccable reputation. It is simply inconceivable that he would choose to crown his career with a fraud. And then, of course, there are the photographs."

"There are pictures?"

"Oh yes. among the numerous illustrations in Garland's book are 10 photographs of crosses and other items from the Parent's original collection."[59]

"Didn't you say something about the medium in this case using a trumpet or megaphone?"

"The way in which spirits spoke through Sophia Williams is a fascinating and evidential story unto itself," he replied. "So fascinating that I didn't mention it in the cases of the crosses because I thought it would distract from the key point that

---

[58] It was Tymn's article in the March 2005 issue of *Fate* magazine that introduced me to Garland's last book. As this is written, he is the editor of the *Academy of Spirituality and Paranormal Studies Bulletin*.

[59] Keith Newlin displays a couple of these photos at: http://www.uncw.edu /garland /gallery /garframe.htm

information known only to the dead was being revealed."

"Now that I have found the evidence truly convincing, can you tell me the rest of the story?"

"Sure can. Voices from the other side could be heard in Sophia Williams' presence as high-pitched, but clear, whispers. Sometimes they seemed to emanate from her chest, sometimes from nearby objects, and sometimes from the empty air above her head, but the spirits did not use her vocal chords or tongue. This was well demonstrated on numerous occasions when researchers held their hands over her mouth or taped it shut while the voices continued unabated."

"Do you mean that Garland and his stenographer and whomever had to sit very close to Williams to hear these voices?"

"At first they did. This is where the trumpet was utilized. They found that they could hear best when Williams held the large end to her chest and Garland listened at the small end, as if using a stethoscope to hear the voices. Then Garland got the idea that he might be able to use a microphone and amplifier to better hear the voices. He shopped around and found an early version of an intercom that consisted of two boxes connected with 60 feet of wire. This mechanism allowed him to sit in his study and listen to the voices emanating from the medium sitting several rooms away. Thus amplified, the spirits could be heard clearly by anyone in the room. What made this set-up so convincing was that the conversations flowed smoothly between the spirits and Garland even though the transmission was one way. Williams could not hear Garland unless he depressed a button on his end of the intercom."

"Let me get this picture perfectly clear," I said. "Garland and, I would assume, one or two of his friends and family, are sitting in a room in his house listening to voices coming from this newfangled gizmo. The voices answer some question of Garland's and then he presses a button on the ... "

"Nope," he interrupted, "he never pressed the button unless he wanted to talk with the medium herself. Williams could not hear Garland's questions or commentary to the spirits."

"So, in order to carry on an intelligible conversation, the spirits of the padres and whomever must have been able to hear Garland directly. They then replied via the medium in another room. That is most unusual, indeed, and most impressive! Was she alone?" I asked.

"Most of the time, Garland's wife or some other person sat with Williams. None of them ever heard the voices while the spirits spoke to Garland through the intercom."

"What was Williams doing while all this communicating was going on?"

"Often she would sit and read a book or magazine."

I wondered: "Did she have to hold the transmitter to her chest?"

"No. Sometimes she held it in her lap, but it seemed to work just as well sitting on a table beside her."

"Could she hear the voices then?"

"At times she heard a few voices, but she believed that the spirits were teaching themselves to use the transmitter directly."

"I can see why you didn't include this information in your cases," I said. "A unique ability such as that would indeed have been a distraction from the already amazing proof of the crosses."

"Unusual, yes, but not unique," he said, and gestured once again towards the manual.

Case 17 – The Ghosts in the Machines

The interaction of departed spirits with electronic equipment was first suspected almost immediately after the invention of electronic equipment. Thomas Edison revealed in 1920 that he was developing equipment to communicate with the spirit world.[60]

If Edison ever accomplished that trick, he chose not to share his contraption with the world at large. Nevertheless, there have been a few successful attempts to augment man's natural ability with electronic devices. One of these was Hamlin Garland's success in using an

[60] See the October 1920 issue of *Scientific American* magazine.

intercom-like device to amplify the direct voices of medium Sophia Williams. Most of the attempts have involved trying to capture voices of the deceased on magnetic audio tape. More recently, some experimenters have tried for voices and/or pictures using videotape and TVs — as sensationalized in the 2005 movie *White Noise*.

The field has long been referred to as "EVP" (standing for Electronic Voice Phenomena) although recently the acronym ITC (for Instrumental TransCommunication) is often preferred. In 1956, the first voices from unknown sources were recorded by Attila von Szalay. Psychical investigators D. Scott Rogo and Raymond Bayless, among others, worked with Szalay and agreed that the voices seem to have a paranormal source. It must be noted that Szalay previously had exhibited mediumistic talents.[61] Soon thereafter, a filmmaker named Friedrich Jügenson heard human voices while playing back some bird songs he had recorded. He ultimately wrote two books on the subject, one of which was read by Konstantin Raudive, a Latvian psychologist. Raudive went on to tape over 70,000 voices he considered to be of paranormal origin and wrote his own book, *Breakthrough*, which was translated into English in 1971. Since then, tens of thousands of people have taken up the pursuit of spirit voices. One of many organizations for practitioners and interested parties, the American Association - Electronic Voice Phenomena, was estab-

---

[61] Estep, p. 14.

lished in 1982 by Sarah Estep, author of the book *Voices of Eternity*.

The process of taping these other-worldly comments consists of turning on a tape recorder, asking a question, allowing the tape to run for a few moments and then rewinding the tape and playing it to see if any voices have been recorded other than your own.

Most of the communications recorded on tape are notable for their brevity, as if each word spoken required a great expenditure of energy. Aside from their presumed origin, they tend to be rather trivial. In the opinion of several critics who have looked into the matter, most of the messages are more the product of a mind that strongly desires to hear voices amongst a background of static than they are of discarnate personalities. This is probably an accurate appraisal. But then there are those pesky exceptions.

The most impressive contemporary example of communications with the other side that are enabled/facilitated by electronic instrumentation is the Spiricom.[62] This box of transistors, resistors, and otheristors was developed by George Meek, William O'Neill, George Mueller, and "Doc Nick." Meek was an engineer whose many patents, mostly in the field of air treatment, generated sufficient income for him to retire at the age of 60 and devote his life and fortune to

---

[62] See the article "Spiricom: Electronic Communications with the 'Dearly Departed'!" by George W. Meek, in *New Realities* magazine, Vol IV, No. 6, July 1982. Additional material may be found in Fuller's *The Ghost of 29 Megacycles*.

psychical research. O'Neill was an electronic technician who seemed able to see and hear dead people. Mueller held a Ph.D. in experimental physics from Cornell University. Doc Nick was a medical doctor and ham-radio operator. At the time they participated in the development of the Spiricom, both Mueller and Nick had been dead for several years.

Rather than rely on deciphering static or "white noise," the Spiricom generates 13 tones that the spirits can manipulate to create the sounds of human language. After much tinkering and many false starts, the team achieved the first real-time, recordable dialog between living and deceased on the 27th of October, 1977. In this breakthrough exchange, the spirit calling himself Doc Nick makes about 15 statements, a couple of which are unintelligible and all of which sound as if he is talking from the bottom of a copper cavern. By the time Meek made his public announcement in 1982, the quality of the voices had been improved significantly; they still sounded metallic and the hum of the overtones was still bothersome, but most everyone could understand the voices upon hearing the tapes but once.

As for verifiable material, the spirit of Mueller provided specifics about his background and education, even his social security number! Furthermore, he gave Meek two unlisted telephone numbers that proved to be for the persons he identified — persons who were exceedingly interested to know how Meek had obtained their "classified" numbers. Here's an excerpt from a tape of a Spiricom-enabled conversation in which the spirit of Mueller asks about a book that he had written in 1947 entitled *Introduction to Electronics*. Earlier, Mueller had suggested that the team refer to a copy of this book.

Mueller: Did you obtain that book of mine yet?

O'Neil: Oh, that book of yours. No sir. By the way, our friend Mr. Meek is really going all out to find that because I want to read those two pages you mentioned.

Mueller: Very well. And I want you to read that, William. There must be copies available somewhere.

O'Neil: Well, I think George, that's Mr. Meek, our friend.

Mueller: *Your* friend.

O'Neil: Yes. Even if he has to go to the Library of Congress. He'll probably do that.

Mueller: Oh, I see. Oh, all right.

Meek later reported: "No, even the Library of Congress does not have a copy. However, I eventually located the book in the archives of the State Historical Society of Wisconsin, Dr. Mueller's native state."

Several voice analyses were done on the tapes. They all showed that the voices of O'Neil and Mueller were of quite different origin. As of this writing, some of these recordings may be heard at www.ghostpix.com.

Doc Nick stopped speaking to O'Neil soon after his voice was caught on tape. After participating in over 30 hours of taped conversations George Mueller ceased to come through. (He had warned the researchers a couple of times that he would not be able to stay with them forever.) O'Neil passed on in 1995, Meek in the winter of '99.

Although Meek had made his fortune with patents, he refused to apply for one on the Spiricom, choosing instead to offer the plans to anyone who wished to replicate his work. It became clear, however, that the Spiricom was an instrument attuned to the unique energies of O'Neil, Nick, and Mueller; it never worked for anyone else on either side of the great divide. Nevertheless, others have had moderate success with different instrumentation and many continue to labor in the ITC field.[63]

End Case 17

"This is the cherry atop the whipped cream on top of the icing on the cake," I commented. "Hardly necessary, but always nice to have more proof of Survival."

"You don't think it could be a hoax?" he asked.

"Well, fraud is theoretically possible, but I can't imagine a motive. Certainly it wasn't for the money. On the other hand, I can't entirely rule out the idea that someone on the outside was playing tricks on the researchers."

"There's a motive problem with that, too," he pointed out. "Why would someone spend months collecting personal data about this Mueller fellow,

---

[63] See Mark Macy's website: http://www.world itc.org/

including his Social Security number, two unlisted telephone numbers he knew, and the fact that he was the author of a most obscure training manual, and then spend more months staying up until the wee hours of the morning carefully doling out bits and pieces of information via super ESP?"

"I can't imagine a motive for such an effort, but why are we talking ESP?" I asked. "Wouldn't some sort of radio transmission have done the job?"

"No. Most of the verifiable information on Mueller was given directly, during the development stage of the Spiricom. At that time, O'Neil could 'hear' Mueller's voice only in his mind; it was not coming through on speakers and did not register on tape. Most of the post-Spiricom, taped conversations — although astounding — are rather tedious, consisting of about what you'd expect from two engineers fine-tuning a piece of equipment.

"All of which strengthens the case, for it would have been sensible — and, no doubt, irresistible — for a charlatan to have put the telephone numbers and such on the tapes."

"Do you think anyone will ever invent an inter-dimensional communicator that works without the need for a human medium?"

"Let's hope not."

I gave him a questioning look.

"Would you really want a spirit telephone sitting beside your living-room couch?" he asked. "Sure it would be cool to call up Helen of Troy and ask if she really loved Paris in the springtime. Or, you could give Professor Einstein a ring when you're having relative trouble. And, wouldn't it be nice to ask Mr. Capone where he stashed his loot?

"But most of us felt guilty that we didn't call mom or grandma often enough when they just lived across town; imagine the burden of knowing that every long-dead great uncle and great-great-grandfather is hoping you'll take a moment to talk!"

"I hadn't really thought of it quite … "

"And don't forget," he went on, " telephones work both ways. Tired of getting calls from living people who want your money or your patronage? Just wait until every spirit with a debt to settle or an axe to grind starts ringing you up a 3 a.m."

Well, I … "

"Have you ever told an obnoxious caller to go to hell? That won't help anymore — they'll just call from there!"

Somewhat overwhelmed by such an idea, I managed to say only: "It's going to take a while for me to absorb all this."

"While your mind is doing its thing, let's go get something for our tummies to absorb," he suggested. "I thought we'd take a ride up to the Panorama, its not too far and the food is almost as good as the view."

I quickly agreed and closed the manual for the day.

As we drove, we got onto the subject of mistakes — why mediums or spirits make mistakes and what that means for the evidential value of their testimony. I didn't record that conversation, but later I wrote a brief paper on the subject that includes much of what we discussed plus a couple of points I thought of later. It seems appropriate to insert that document next in place of our rather mundane dinner conversation.

Saturday Supper Substitute

Inhuman Perfection?

Oh, if I could only leave you the proof that I continue. ... I am trying, amid unspeakable difficulties. ... The nearest simile I can find to express the difficulty of sending a message is that I appear to be standing behind a sheet of frosted glass, which blurs sight and deadens sound, dictating feebly to a reluctant and somewhat obtuse secretary.

— The spirit of F.W.H. Myers[64]

When a medium gets no message, or when a message seems inaccurate, in whole or in part, critics often claim that these "failures" taint all the evidence and, therefore, nothing has been proven. Such a view is both unfair and unreasonable.

There are at least four and often five or more parties involved in a mediumistic communication. Let's consider them one at a time, beginning with the "control."

---

[64] *Proceedings of the Society of Psychical Research*, vol. xxi. p. 230.

The Control

Not all mediums (and I include channelers in this term) have an obvious control and some controls claim to be extensions of the medium's subconscious, but most mediums who go into a trance during a sitting seem to be taken over by a discarnate entity who claims to be an independent person — a human much like you and I, who just happens to be dead. The truth probably lies somewhere in between; one possibility being that the control personality is an *ad hoc* amalgam of the medium's brain and one or more spirit minds.

Now, the process of dying may be somewhat enlightening, but it can also be frightening and confusing. We have no evidence that dying changes one's personality or intellect. It doesn't make you nicer and it doesn't make you smarter. It doesn't make you more honest, or less prone to exaggeration, or less hungry for adulation. And it most certainly doesn't make you omnipotent or incapable of making mistakes.

All human beings make mistakes, including me. I've been known to say 'west' when I meant 'east,' thus causing folks to waste a lot of time driving in the wrong direction. I've even been known to call my good friend "Dave" when his name is "Joe." I've written the wrong total on a deposit slip, purchased the wrong brand of soap, and sometimes I have no idea where I parked my car. Chances are that you, being human, have made similar mistakes. All people do. And being dead doesn't change that.

Likewise, dying doesn't expunge the natural human tendencies to exaggerate a little to make a better impression and to fill in story gaps with a bit of fabrication. Much fuss has been made over one of Piper's controls providing messages from a persona named "Bessie Beals" — a name invented by the sitter as a test. Even though the control admitted making a mistake, some critics act as if this one incident somehow negates the three decades of solid proof provided by Piper's various controls. To me, such a display of "human" frailty only adds to the authenticity of the process.

Thus, it is neither surprising nor calamitous to occasionally catch a control being less than honest or less than perfect.

The Contacts

What is characteristic of a control is even more true of the contacts (the souls that are being contacted during the sitting). In most cases, these people are fairly new to the spirit condition. Often, they were not expecting to die and many are surprised to find themselves still aware. They will likely be more enthusiastic than the control about the prospect of speaking to a loved one who is still "in body." All this leads to uncertainty, confusion, and agitation, a sure recipe for blunders in communication.

For both controls and contacts, the way in which they gather information must also be taken into account, particularly when asked to monitor someone who is living (as in "What is so-and-so doing now?"). One of the more common mistakes spirits make is the misidentification of country or other geographic demarcation — confusing America with Australia, for instance. But how does one identify a country? As I sit writing this, I look out my office window and see no indication of what country or state I am in. The clouds do not spell out "U.S.A.," the street below is not stamped boldly with "Pennsylvania." To a spirit drawn to a person by name, and looking around in that person's vicinity, parts of America look very like parts of Australia. Given time to search about, a higher accuracy might be attainable, but in the rapid fire Q-and-A characteristic of many sittings, a few geographical mix-ups are to be expected.

Another troublesome area for spirits seems to be time frame. On numerous occasions, spirits asked to report on an earthbound person's activities will provide a lengthy and detailed report that is absolutely wrong for the time specified but absolutely correct for another time (such as an hour earlier or the day before). On the one hand, I don't suppose we should be surprised if time doesn't run quite the same way in the next world as it does in this one. On the other hand, the problem could well lie, once again, in the way in which information is obtained. If a spirit knows what we are doing by tapping into our mental pictures of the action, this sort of chronological displacement would be expected. After all, we don't time-stamp our memories.

Historical time can also be problematic. Sometimes the only way to tell what year it is, or even what century, is by asking about historical events. But occasionally even this approach fails. Marge Rieder reports that once, when she instructed a patient "to go back in time to the Civil War, the patient immediately began describing a lifetime during the French Revolution."[65]

A third type of information that spirits often have trouble communicating is persons' names. Often mediums receive a name in bits and pieces, perhaps an initial and then some symbol. The process reminds me very much of a game of charades. The name "Rose" is fairly easy to symbolize, but "Robert" or "Jerry" is a much greater challenge. For those mediums who receive much of their information via pictures, symbols, gestures, and other such impressions, some difficulty with names is to be expected.

Also, spirits sometimes confuse the living and the dead, an error likewise made by some during NDEs. Critics often reject cases solely because a claim is made that the spirit of a living person was seen along with the spirits of those who have crossed over. What these critics seem to forget is that the differences we so easily note between the corporeal and the astral may not be nearly so apparent when viewed from the other side. To a spirit, all people may appear as light forms, with only minor details to distinguish whether they still reside in the flesh or not. NDErs and others who are new to the game should be excused if they sometimes miss those details.

Difficulties are not limited to knowledge of other people and foreign places. It is perfectly natural for all people, living and dead, to forget even those personal

---

[65] Rieder, *Mission to Millboro*, p. xvii.

things that others remember well. Sir Oliver Lodge recounts a most revealing incident along these lines. He once asked his children to play a game in which they were to pretend that he had died and that a medium claimed to be in touch with his spirit. The children were to test the spirit by asking questions that their father should be able to answer. But when the children asked their questions, Lodge found that he and they had totally different ideas of what incidents were significant in his life. He could not answer a single one of their questions. Finally he exclaimed in mock despair: "That settles it. I am not your father!"[66]

The Medium

Now we consider the person whose body is clearly essential to the process. But the mind of the medium also seems to play a role. Even when in trance, some sort of translation process is occurring that is more or less dependent upon the medium's vocabulary and memories. This allows some room for error. Those mediums who remain awake and aware throughout the process are even more subject to making natural human mistakes in translating the symbols and feelings they receive into understandable sentences. They also must ignore the biases and assumptions of their conscious mind and are more subject to distractions and false feedback from others in the room, both in body and in spirit.

The Recorder

These days, the more scientific and evidential attempts at spirit communication are video-recorded,

---

[66] Spraggett, *Arthur Ford*, p. 94.

but many of the greatest mediums of the past were recorded only when someone in attendance was handed a pad and pencil and asked to take notes. We are safe in assuming that such folks were rarely perfect in their transcriptions. Being like the rest of us, a recorder would tend to hear what he or she expected. Some of their mistakes must have resulted in hits being counted as misses; although, to be fair, some misses were likely counted as hits.

The Sitter

And finally, we consider the person who has come for a reading by the medium. They too are subject, of course, to all the human frailties mentioned above. In addition to such, there is the problem of non-correction. Over and over, the scholar comes across cases wherein a sitter claims some information to be wrong and then later recants because they remember a forgotten person or are corrected as to a falsely held belief (*i.e.* grandma says that the house actually *was* blue, or Jim really did go to Michigan not Michigan State, or there was a sister who died at birth, or some such thing). Often, these corrections are not made until days or months after the reading took place. Knowing the human disposition toward laziness and forgetfulness, one can safely assume that many corrections that ought to be made never happen; thus, leaving false "mistakes" on the record.

Some skeptics might claim that this distortion of results is counterbalanced by the sitter's natural inclination to accept statements that are ambiguous. No doubt it is true that, in general commerce, sitters tend to be gullible, that they provide too much information to the medium and are too ready to count vague responses as solid hits. But in the cases that qualify for our consideration, the opposite is true. Researchers and sitters today and their fellows who investigated the great mediums of prior centuries were and are, on the whole, extremely suspicious and dubious. Today's scoring methods are clearly unfavorable to the mediums, yet the results still indicate communication from the deceased.

Thus, we must realize that all humans make mistakes and that the process of dying does not involve being sprayed with perfect juice. Errors in readings can hardly be avoided. In fact, too many mistake-free readings would be good cause for suspicion of fakery.

Faking It

Speaking of fakery, it should be pointed out that an occasional deceit is just as human as an occasional mistake. It is hardly surprising, then, to discover that mediums are not necessarily always perfectly honest.

A medium with a reputation to uphold is under a lot of pressure to perform consistently. Yet the mechanisms of their performance are just as mysterious to them as to their audience. Mediums are totally dependent on forces and spirits beyond their control. What job could be more stressful? The temptation is strong to do a bit of research so that a few facts will be available in case the spirits fail to deliver. Some mediums, being human, have succumbed to this temptation.

The famous medium Arthur Ford, for example, was discovered to possess a suitcase of news clippings that may have helped him in his "readings" of well-known people. But this discovery does not reduce the evidential value of Ford's many impressive performances under conditions that obviated the possibility of prior research.[67]

For this reason, any evidence of research should remove from consideration whatever could conceivably be obtained from research, but should not affect the evidentiary value of information impossible to obtain via research.

Non-Contact

Even getting some misinformation is preferable to getting no information at all. Sometimes a medium is criticized, even castigated, for being unable to contact the sought after spirit. Often the medium is not to blame. There are several possible reasons, quite beyond human control, for a failure to reach the other side. A spirit may have already returned to a physical body or may have advanced to levels beyond the reach of the medium. A spirit may not want to spoil your fun, relieve the suspense, or whatever. And, just because one is a spirit, doesn't necessarily mean one has an interest in talking to the living. As the psychoanalyst Nandor Fodor has opined: "Frankly, I don't think the dead care too much about us, for the simple reason that we are not too upset about the troubles of kindergarten children. ... It would be much more important and interesting, surely,

---

[67] See, for example, the sitting in Upton Sinclair's home (Spraggett, *Arthur Ford*, pp. 227-230).

to explore the possibilities of the after-death state than to worry about the possibilities of the life left behind."[68]

---

[68] Spraggett, *The Unexplained*, p.199

Saturday Night

How This Could Be

This room and all the atmosphere around you right now is full of people and full of voices ... but until you turn on the TV you can't see and hear them, can you? Well, that's the way we are. It's just another dimension, another wavelength, so to speak.
— Fletcher[69]

The night was clear but warmer when we got back to the cabin so, after letting Dasher out for a twilight run, we forswore the fireplace for the fireflies and went back to our chairs on the long, narrow screened porch.

"I was thinking last evening that this really is almost heaven," I said, as I settled back and patted my too full belly.

"I reckon you mean West Virginia," he smiled, "but you'd be correct no matter where you were on earth."

---

[69] Spraggett, *Arthur Ford*, p. 59.

"Say again?"

"It's like surfing the Web," he continued, "no matter where you are you're only one screen away from where you want to be. You just have to know what keys to punch."

"So, heaven is just a click away?"

"Different picture, same monitor.

"In Garland's last book, there is a succinct statement by the discarnate Father Espejo: 'I am not from afar, I am *here*. I am not of the sixteenth century, I am *now*.'[70]

"Heaven, it would seem, is the same place everything is."

"How can that be? Does this have something to do with quantum physics?"

"'Quantum' is a term used — much as 'magnetic' and 'electric' were used a century or so ago — by writers who'd like to believe that the science of the day supports their metaphysical doctrines; but, I wouldn't put much stock in such claims. In the entire world, there might be a score of folks who have a real grasp of quantum physics ... and they rarely agree with one another."

"That reminds me of something I once read by the guy who headed the Fermi accelerator," I said. It went

---

[70] *The Mystery of the Buried Crosses*, Garland, p. 193.

something like: 'We are drowning in theoretical possibilities not based on a single solitary fact.' "[71]

"Yes, and there is an unfortunate tendency for advocates to adopt the latest theoretical possibility as an 'explanation' of their pet concept, while ignoring the lack of factual evidence. If some fellow tells you that ghosts or some such phenomena can be explained by 11-dimensional-string theory, you'd best assume that fellow hasn't the slightest idea what he's talking about."

"So what's your explanation?" I asked.

"I don't pretend to explain anything. I rather doubt that anyone is capable of understanding the real truth. Although we hate to admit it, all the mechanisms of the universe are not necessarily amenable to human language, or even to human thought.

"Did you know that belief in psychic phenomena is greater among the better educated?"[72]

I replied that I was unaware of this fact.

"It's true. And perhaps the reason is that a better informed person can better comprehend the existence of unknowable things.

---

[71] Nobel winner Leon Lederman, Ph.D., quoted in *The Washington Post* article "Physicists Plan World's Largest Atomic Machine" by Philip J. Hilts, 16 August 1983, p. A4, col. 1. Of course, he was arguing for the expenditure of a stupendous amount of money to construct a new accelerator that might reveal some of those missing facts.

[72] Schmicker, p. 18.

"Nevertheless, without some rationale, the evidence for Survival is more difficult to accept. So, if you wish, I can offer a few concepts that might help you understand how it is possible for heaven and earth, and hell also, to exist in the same here and now."

I gave him a "go-right-ahead" motion.

"Let's start with the seemingly unscientific idea of magic mirrors."

"You mean as in 'Who's the fairest of them all?'?"

"The use of mirrors to contact spirits has, indeed, been practiced since before Snow White's time. And, by the way, is still being practiced productively today.[73] But mirrors are magical in a more basic way, for they help us to comprehend the concept of all-in-one. Consider this one here."

"I wondered why that was there." It was a cheaply framed full-length mirror such as you might buy at a discount store. He had mounted it on the cedar siding just outside the door to the porch. "Is that a magic one?"

"As magical as any," he replied. "Look into it and tell me what you see."

I turned and looked into the mirror at the darkening forest: "Just a few trees. Guess I'm not adept at reading mirrors."

---

[73] See *Reunions*, by Moody.

Unperturbed, he asked: "Can you see the tree with the broken limb hanging to the ground."

"Not in the mirror," I said, although I could easily see such a tree off to my other side.

"I can see it quite clearly," he stated, as he stared into the mirror.

"Of course you can; you're at a different angle than I."

"Can you see the entire height of the screen, from floor to ceiling."

"Just barely."

He got up and retrieved a large piece of cardboard that had been cut from a shipping box and leaned it against the mirror, covering the lower half. "Now can you still see the entire screen?"

"No."

"That's strange; I can."

"Okay. I get the point.

"What you can see in a mirror depends on your angle of view. At any given time, there are an uncountable number of views available in that single mirror."

"Correct. And?"

"And, how much you can see in a mirror depends on how close you are."

"What if I were to break the mirror into a dozen pieces and hand you a single fragment? What could you see in that?'

"Well, if I held it close to my eye," I said, demonstrating with the flat of my hand, "I guess I could see most everything."

"Suppose you dropped that piece and it broke into a dozen smaller pieces?"

"I'd have to hold one closer, but I could still see the entire scene within it."

"So the entire scene that you first saw in the whole mirror is actually available in each piece or part of the mirror."

"Yes, I never thought of it before, but mirrors are like 2-dimensional versions of holograms. Or maybe I should say a hologram is like a mirror frozen in time. Wasn't there a book about that?"

"Yes, by Michael Talbot.[74] You should consider reading it.

"So, could it be that our universe is similar to a mirror or a hologram in that all information exists everywhere and what we experience depends solely on our 'point of view'?"

"I don't know, I guess that helps me accept the possibility of multiple universes all in the here and now, but it doesn't give me much sense of why I'm usually aware of only one of them."

"For that, we leave the ancient art of mirror gazing and the advanced science of holography for the more conventional technology of the telephone."

---

[74] *The Holographic Universe*, Talbot.

"Aha," I interjected, "a telephone between worlds."

"That, by the way, is actually the title of another interesting little book,[75] but one that's irrelevant to my point."

"Which is?"

"Which is multiplexing.

"You might be too young to remember having to make sure that none of your neighbors were talking on the 'party line' before you could make a telephone call."

"I was a mere babe, but I remember. You could never be certain that no one was listening to your conversations."

"In my neighborhood," he sighed, "you usually could be certain someone *was* listening.

"Do you recall how you could tell that a call was for your family?"

"The rings were different, weren't they?"

"Right. Calls to one house might be indicated by two short rings separated by a pause. Calls to the house next door, by one long and then one short ring, and so on. A simple code that allowed multiple users to share one copper wire. A very basic form of multiplexing.

"As telephone equipment became more sophisticated, more advanced forms of multiplexing were developed to allow the limited number of lines between cities to handle a growing number of long-

---

[75] *Telephone Between Worlds*, Crenshaw.

distance calls. What happens is that equipment at both ends of the long-distance lines chops several calls into little coded snippets that are interspersed among the bits of other signals and then sent through shared circuits in rapid-fire sequence. At the other end, the pieces are sorted out, reassembled and sent on as complete conversations. The pulses come so quickly that your brain cannot detect the gaps between them and so the transmission sounds smooth and seamless."

"Cool enough, but what does that have to do … "

"If, as some spirits claim, the universe blinks, then it could very well be multiplexed. Myriad, totally different and separate worlds or planes could then all co-exist in the same space."

"The universe blinks?"

"On and off, on and off."

"Uh, where does it go when it's off?"

"When it's off, the idea of 'where' is likewise off."

"You mean it no longer exists at all?"

"Think about a strip of motion picture film. When it is run through a projector, one frame is shown by shining a bright light through it. Then a shutter closes, blocking the light while the film is advanced to the next frame. The shutter opens allowing the light to project the next image and then the process is repeated. At 30 cycles per second, our brains interpret this rush of images as seamless movement.

Now, where do the movie characters go between frames?"

"There's no answer to that," I said, "they don't 'go' anywhere because they don't exist between the frames."

"Back when I went to the movies a lot, there was only one theater per building, but now it seems most movie houses are complexes."

"It's more efficient to have only one ticket booth and lobby and such serve multiple theaters," I pointed out.

"Let's carry that idea a bit further and have one projector serve two theaters."

"And how might that be accomplished?"

"Simply by interspersing one movie, every other frame, among another movie. Then, speed up the projector so that it is showing 60 frames per second instead of 30. Use a rotating mirror synchronized to the projector to direct the frames belonging to one movie into one theater and the frames belonging to the other movie into the other theater."

"That would probably work," I commented, "although it doesn't seem very efficient, and both movies would then have to begin and end at the same time, and the audio track would be tough to handle."

"Well, no analogy is perfect," he shrugged. "The important point is that it doesn't matter how much distance there is between frames. There could be one movie interspersed, or a dozen. As long as the film, the projector, and our brains are synchronized, the illusion of reality is maintained.

"In the same way, there could be many universes blinking into and out of existence in sequence. Our senses would detect only that universe with which we were synchronized. We wouldn't normally notice the blinking. A million or more other universes could come into existence and vanish again with each blink and we might be no more aware of them than the characters in one film would be aware of the characters in another, interspersed, film."

"So, you're saying that the universe is multiplexed and …"

"I'm saying it is *possible*. It would help explain a lot of strange phenomena, especially if our minds and souls were more or less constant."

"You mean that souls don't blink?"

"Again, it would explain much if various aspects of ourselves blinked at different rates. Our brains, being part of the physical universe, would, of course, blink at the same rate as the physical universe. But our minds might be synched with both the physical universe and a mental universe. This could explain where we are when we are dreaming. Then our astral bodies could be synched to blink with the physical, the mental, and the astral universe; thereby spanning all three. And so on, up the pyramid to the Godhead."

"So then, God would be the universal constant; the part that doesn't blink."

"Yep. I reckon you could say that God is always 'on.'"

"That would make a great T-shirt.

"I wonder if there is any way that such a hypothesis could be proved or disproved."

"None that I can think of, although there are numerous reports of anomalous events that could be explained much easier by reference to multiplexing."

"You mean like the folks who claim that they were miraculously transported across an intersection, thus saving them from a collision that was imminent an instant before?"

"Yes, or the many cases of 'missing time' in which people discover that several minutes or hours have passed that they were not aware of."

"Well, whether it explains hiccups in either time or space, I like your analogy."

"Thanks," he smiled, "but most of the credit goes to others."[76]

"The only complaint I have is that 'blinks' sounds like something has been shorted out."

"Would you prefer 'flickers'?"

---

[76] Thanks to Seth, who talks about blinking universes in *The Unknown Reality: Vol I*, pp. 87-88 and in *Seth Speaks*, pp. 133 & 266, and to J.H. Mathes who mentions multiplexed realities in *The Amnesia Factor*, pp. 125-126.

"That's even worse." I thought for a moment and then my eyes lifted to the star-filled sky and I suddenly knew just the term. "How about 'twinkles'?"

He saw where I was looking and smiled. "Okay then, our first analogy for the operation of the multiverse is that it twinkles."

"First? You have more than one?"

"Oh yes, many. But it's getting late," he said, "so we'll just look at one or two others.

"During our walk today, did you notice the bush out where the driveway meets the road?"

"You mean the one with the gorgeous pink flowers?"

"Yes, and the fact that you saw the pink flowers on the green bush indicates that you do not suffer from the most common form of color blindness."

"Yeah, I knew that. I took those tests when I was in school. You know, the ones where you look at a bunch of colored dots and if you can see one number you are color blind and if you see another number you aren't."

"Exactly the response I was seeking! Now, imagine a somewhat larger picture consisting of many thousands of dots of various colors so that a person with red-green color blindness would see the word 'EARTH' and a person with blue-yellow color blindness would see the word 'HEAVEN' while a person with full color vision would see the words 'HEAVEN AND EARTH.'"

"I'm not certain that is technically possible, but I can do that in my imagination."

"Good. Now just make that picture three-dimensional and enlarge it by a factor of a billion-billion or so and you have another way of wrapping your mind around the idea of several different worlds existing, interspersed, within the same space."

I considered this for awhile and then I got an idea that made me convulse with one of those hrrummf-snort-giggle combinations, and he asked what was so funny. And I sighed and said, "Well, I was thinking of all those little colored dots distributed throughout the universe like sprinkles on ice cream and it occurred to me that the two grand analogies you've offered for the comprehension of our universe can be summarized in two words: 'twinkle' and 'sprinkle.'"

He grinned broadly, shook his head slightly, and said: "I reckon that's all we're likely to accomplish this evening. Tomorrow we consider what heaven is actually like."

And so, muttering and chuckling to ourselves, we made our way to bed.

Sunday Morning I

Time for Breakfast

*Here we are, set in the midst of an infinity of time
... the chances are infinitely against us that we
should be alive at any specific time. But here we
are. The only way to get rid of the infinity of
chances which are against us is to assume ... that
we too are infinite.*

— J. Paul Williams,
Essay in the *Yale Review*, Spring, 1945

We enjoyed our breakfast of fruit cup and French toast
out at the small table on the screened porch. The aroma
of coffee mixing with the fresh scents of summertime in
the woods made for a most pleasant morning. Apparently it put him in a speculative mood.

"Let's say that I asked you to meet me on the
corner of Twelfth Street and Vine," he said, as he
poured himself some apple juice. "And you agreed,
but I went and stood on the corner and you failed
to meet me. Assume also that we do actually meet
again, say ... in the lobby of the Hotel California,

and I ask you why you failed to show up. What excuse would you offer?"

"Well, you never said which 'Twelfth Street and Vine,' but I well remember the song,[77] so I'm 'going to Kansas City' … Missouri, that is."

"Yep," he agreed, "that's where I was."

"The question, then, is *when* were you standing on that corner? I was there at 3 p.m. and you were no where to be seen."

"Aha!" he exclaimed, with a bit more enthusiasm than needed. "That explains it. I was there at 2 o'clock.

"We were missing an entire dimension!"

"I've never been real comfortable with the idea of time as a dimension," I said.

"Dimensions are simply labels we use to identify places," he explained.

"I thought they were how we measured the size of things," I replied, "like length, width, and height."

"The size of a thing is calculated or *derived* from its dimensions. For example, to determine the length of that log," he gestured towards a large dead limb on the forest floor, "you would first need to have a starting point and an ending point and then calculate the difference between the two. If you were

---

[77] Wilbert Harrison's *Kansas City* made the Top Ten in 1959. If you want to stand there too, you'll have to use some imagination, as the streets no longer intersect in Kansas City, MO.

using a tape measure, your starting point would be zero and your ending point would be whatever number on the tape coincided with the other end of the log. But you could also derive the length of the log using the longitude and latitude of the two ends and a bit of elementary trigonometry."

"Perhaps *you* could," I said, "there's nothing about trigonometry that I consider elementary.

"I do know that longitude and latitude are numbers signifying a certain distance from the Greenwich meridian and the equator. And, I suppose that the corner of Twelfth Street and Vine is distinguished from the corner of Eleventh Street and Vine by its distance from First Street. But, I still am confused about dimensions and size and time."

"The difficulty arises from our use of the term 'dimension' to mean both scale and size. When we say that the dimensions of a rectangle are 4 inches by 6 inches, we are talking about size or quantity. On the other hand, when we say that there are three dimensions in space, we are referring to directions. These directions can be given mathematically according to the x, y, and z axes; or, on a geological map, by longitude, latitude, and height above sea level; or, in everyday terms, as up-down, right-left, and forward-back.

"So, from now on, when we want to talk about length and width or some other indication of size, let's speak of 'proportions' or simply 'size' and reserve the term 'dimensions' for information that tells us where something is on a particular spatial scale."

"And the scale time is on … ?"

"Exactly."

"Exactly? Exactly what?"

"The scale of time is on."

" … Uh, pardon me, but have we slipped into an Abbott and Costello reject?"

"On, as opposed to off," he said with a grin. "Remember what we said last night about the universe blinking, or rather 'twinkling' on and off?"

"Yes."

"Think of each 'on' blink to be one unit of time. Let's call that a 'twink.'"

I was pretty certain he was making this up as he went along, but I just said: "Okay. How long is a twink?"

"A twink is an indivisible unit. It cannot be divided into smaller parts; therefore, its duration is zero."

"So then, no time passes during a twink? How does anything happen?"

"For the universe to actually blink, or twinkle, it would have to be constantly re-created. Movement, or change, comes about because each new creation is a tiny bit different than the previous one.

"Think again of the movie frames. Each frame is static, a still picture. The action in the movie we see is the result of each succeeding frame being different from the last. The main difference between the film analogy and 'reality' is that each twink of the universe has been created fresh, rather than being preordained by the producer."

"So, movement occurs only when the universe is off?"

"No. When the universe is off, physical objects do not exist, so they cannot move. In fact, nothing ever really 'moves.' At each twink, all things are created anew, only in a slightly different position than they were in the preceding twink."

"Just how rapidly does the universe twinkle?" I asked while pouring extra syrup on my French toast.

"That's like asking the characters in a movie to tell you the speed of the projector. We denizens of the physical universe cannot detect the twinks. You would need to be on the outside of the system to do that. Nevertheless, based on Planck's constant, we can assume that the minimum number of twinks that occur in each second of our time is very large."

"How large?" I asked.

"So large that there is no English word for the number, although I believe it could be termed 'one quintillion septillion.' Physicists write it as 10^{43}, if you wrote it out it would be the number one followed by 43 zeros."

"Do you expect me to believe that the entire universe is terminated and regenerated one-quintillion-septillion times each second?"

"If you can accept that something was created once, is it so much harder to believe that it was, and is still, being created many times?

"Perhaps the British astronomer and physicist Sir Arthur Eddington was correct when he said: 'Not once in the dim past, but continuously by conscious mind is the miracle of the Creation wrought.'" [78]

"Aha. ... Excuse me for asking, but how do you know all this?"

"I don't. It's just speculative extrapolation. Remember that the whole 'universe blinks' thing was introduced as an analogy to help us understand certain possibilities." He took a sip of coffee.

"But whether our world actually blinks or twinkles or whatever, time is still a dimension because time is a way of locating things in space. Or, rather, time is a way to determine *what* space we are locating things within."

I must have looked a bit befuddled, because he said: "Let's go back to Kansas City. The Twelfth and Vine where I was standing had a blue Edsel parked on the corner. Did you see it?"

"No," I played along, "just a Studebaker and a 1950 Nash Rambler. You know, the kind that the seats folded back into a bed."

---

[78] Eddington Arthur, *The Nature of the Physical World*, The University of Michigan Press, 1978, p. 241.

"There's an old fella up the hill still has one of those sitting out in his front yard. No tires on it, but the bed still works. I think he sleeps in it when it gets too hot indoors.

"Anyway, the space in which I was waiting to meet you had a blue Edsel on the corner; the space where you came to meet me had a Nash Rambler instead. We are clearly referring to two different Twelfth and Vines."

"But we'll never meet if we have to make dates according to what cars are on the corner. That blue Edsel might be there every afternoon, but it might not."

"Which is precisely why a device that produces nothing and transforms nothing is, nevertheless, one of mankind's most important inventions."

"Clocks?"

"Of course. All that clocks do is move in a constant and reliable fashion — unlike the traffic in Kansas City. This allows me to say: 'I'll be standing on the corner of Twelfth Street and Vine at 2 p.m.,' and you will know that I am specifying one particular intersection out of all the gazillion Twelfth & Vines that there have been in the past and will be in the future. I am not talking about the intersection at which the clock's hands point to 3 or 4 or 5. I am specifying that singular Twelfth Street and Vine at which the little hand of the clock is pointing to the 2. And it doesn't matter if the car on the corner is a blue Edsel or a yellow Hummer.

"Time is not something that changes; time is just a scale we use to locate events."

"In that case," I said, "it really makes no sense to speak of the flow of time or the passage of time, does it?"

"No more sense than it makes to talk about the flow of latitude or the passage of depth."

"Then, do you think time travel is possible?" I asked.

"Once an event has occurred, I very much doubt that it can be undone," he replied while stacking our empty plates. "On the other hand, it would be imprudent of me to surmise any constraints on what could take place in the gaps between twinks."

"What about the future? Can spirits foretell the future?"

"I doubt that even God knows the future."

"Then you don't believe Him omniscient?" I asked.

"To know all doesn't mean knowing what is not," he replied. "Knowledge comes only from experience — it can be the experience of doing, or sensing, or just thinking. There can be no knowledge if the experience has not occurred."

Apparently sensing my dissatisfaction with this idea, he went on: "For anyone, even God, to know anything, there must be some experience of it. And for Him to have experienced something, it must have already happened. To know the future, therefore, would require going through the process twice. I hardly think that the Almighty would have nothing better to do than repeat experiences that He has already had. And, even if He did repeat Himself, what of the initial experience? There's a first time for everything — even for God."

"Well," I said, "could it not be that God knows the future because He has thought it through, and now we are living it?"

"Ah my friend," he sighed. "What are we, but the thoughts of God? And, what is our living, but God experiencing Himself in the form of the world?"

At this point, I switched off my recorder, my experience having shown that it was useless in picking up conversations over the sounds of table clearing and dish washing.

Sunday Morning II

Other Lives

In every generation for more than 10,000 years, man has been given overpowering evidence that his personality will survive death. The authenticity of this evidence becomes more convincing the more carefully it is observed. There is no rational reason why a general acceptance of the fact of survival should be delayed any longer.

— Jerome Ellison[79]

After breakfast we found that the wind had picked up considerably making the porch a less than attractive setting, so we adjourned to the recliners in the main room.

"Both the ancient Egyptians and the Tibetans created well-known 'Books of the Dead'" he said, "intended to guide the soul on its journey to the afterlife. To the extent that these tomes have

---

[79] Epilogue to *The Life Beyond Death*, by Arthur Ford, p. 169

influenced the beliefs of readers, they may well have affected the souls' postmortem experiences. This is because in heaven, even more than on physical worlds, what you expect or believe affects what you experience.

"Much of what we know about heaven comes from the descriptions obtained during hypnotic regressions to the time before birth. Thousands of such regressions have been performed. We can rely on this testimony to the extent that it matches the descriptions given by other people likewise regressed. (If everybody is telling the same story, then that story is probably true, providing, of course, that outside influences have been ruled out.)

"Our knowledge of the afterlife also comes from its current residents (discarnate souls) via mediums. Some of these souls, we should note, have expressed concern that the process of interpreting their reality in physical terms cannot be accomplished without considerable distortion.[80]

"Altogether, hundreds of people have made important additions to our current understanding.

"Any questions before we delve into the heavenly environs?"

"I am now certain that there is an afterlife," I said, "but I'm not real clear on *what* it is that survives."

"Then allow me to try and clarify the situation," he replied. "That which is 'you' is a one-of-a-kind, one-time-only combination of your physical body and a

---

[80] For example, see White, *The Betty Book*, p. 109.

portion of your soul. Your physical body will die and decompose, your brain along with it. Your physical body *will* not be, *can* not be resurrected. [If you disagree, consider that the molecules that now make up your body have formed the structure of other persons in the past.] Thus, no life is lived twice, which means that what is now *you* will not 'live again.'

"But your soul will not die with your body. That portion of your soul that currently resides within your body will be set free and will return to its wholeness in heaven. Your soul will remember being you, as it remembers being all of the entities it has been part of throughout the ages."

I said, "I take it you believe in reincarnation."

"If you don't, you haven't honestly evaluated the evidence," he replied.

"Way back when, I did read the book about Bridey Murphy and I remember being impressed, but I heard that had been discredited."

"There certainly was no dearth of critics of Morey Bernstein's *The Search for Bridey Murphy*. And some strange bedfellows they made, too. The atheists, of course, were against it, as were those whose religions do not offer second chances. Tucked in with them, to the surprise of many, were more than a few ardent spiritualists who weren't enthusiastic about normal folk being able to contact spirits on their own."

"But Bridey wasn't a departed spirit," I pointed out.

"Many mediums claimed she was. Despite what their own spirit contacts were teaching, these mediums denied reincarnation, asserting that, rather than being recalled from a past life, the memories were those of deceased spirits being telepathically transmitted to the entranced subject."

"That's a bit of a stretch. But I suppose everybody tends to see things according to their own beliefs."

"A tendency against which we must be constantly vigilant," he said. "Anyway, it turns out that the so-called refutation of the Bridey Murphy case is, itself, full of holes. The 1965 edition of the book showed that emphatically. Of course, I can't blame you for not knowing this; you can bet that long after the public forgets the truth, the überskeptics will continue to repeat the fabrications.

"I suggest you re-read Bernstein's book; it is both entertaining and convincing. The sessions revealed an impressive number of details about the culture Bridey knew in Ireland, details she had no way of knowing in her current life and that could only be confirmed by painstaking research. Nevertheless, it was hardly the first or last good treatise on reincarnation. Solid evidence has been known for centuries, and even stronger evidence continues to be found to this day."

"Didn't the early Christians believe in reincarnation?"

"For over 500 years, many did, including some very prominent leaders. But then, the petty tyrants — who felt that the threat of eternal damnation was critical to the church's control of its members — won the debate. From then on, believers in reincarnation were branded (and often executed) as heretics."

"But, what about the argument that everyone could not have lived on earth before, because there are more humans alive today than have lived in all our past history — there just aren't enough past lives to go around."

"True enough," he replied, "but that was also true at mankind's beginning. Clearly the first people on earth could not have been reincarnated souls, as they had no predecessors. And their immediate children, at the least, were likewise souls unaccustomed to the earthly plane.

"But, who knows how many souls there are in the universe, either incarnated on other worlds or simply hanging around heaven. Probably more than enough to inhabit many times the number of bodies this planet can hold."

"Good point," I conceded. "I hadn't thought of that. But, if we accept that many people have lived numerous past lives and factor in the recent population growth, then a large segment (maybe even the majority) of those now living on earth are here for the first time."

"Perhaps."

"Why just 'perhaps'? It doesn't add up any other way."

"Well now, I can think of at least three factors that would change your equation. The first is that no one can say for sure how many people *have* lived on Earth. There could well have been extensive populations that pre-date our earliest records."

"You mean Atlantis and Mu?" I queried.

"I mean that our planet is very old and holds many mysteries. Until we solve them all, let's not discount the possibility of unknown civilizations.

"The second possibility," he continued, "is that souls might be able to split as they grow, as do the roots of a tree. If so, then the soul of one ancient forefather might now be incarnated in several current residents of Earth."

"Then two people under hypnosis might be induced to remember the same life," I speculated.

"In theory, although I've heard of no such incident."

"And what's the third factor I might have missed?"

"Ah," he hesitated a moment, "well, that's the one I am least comfortable with ... transmigration."

"You mean coming back as an animal?" I exclaimed.

"No. I mean coming *from* an animal. Some cultures fervently believe that souls develop by incarnating first in lower life forms and graduating to higher and more intelligent species as they grow."

"The idea doesn't feel right to me," I said.

"Me neither; but, is our resistence to it based on it being false or simply on human pride? Whatever the case, I've not seen any solid evidence for the reality of it.

"Is something on your mind?"

Apparently he had noticed that distant look I get when impressed by an odd idea. After a moment of thought collection, I said: "Just thinking about the spiritualist viewpoint. Knowing as we do that spirits of deceased humans exist, and that they could well be capable of imparting their memories to humans, how can we tell if a particular experience stemmed from reincarnation or from possession?"

"Indeed, I don't know what the criteria for making such a decision would be. But the fact that spirit possession might account for the reception of any particular information about another life, is not an argument against reincarnation. Just because we can't tell whether something comes from source A or source B, is no proof that there is no source B."

"Granted.

"So, out of all the volumes of evidence that must exist for the soul living more than one physical life, which have you put in your little blue book?" I said, reaching once again for the *Afterlife Casebook*.

"There are a few cases there that appertain. Go ahead and take a look."

And so I did.

Case 18 – Hypnotist's Heaven

There are many reasons for the increase over the past century in the quantity and quality of evidence for Survival. Medical advances, better communications, and faster ambulances have led to far more resuscitations of people who would otherwise have died, thus leading to many more near-death experiences; hospitalizations of the very ill are more common, resulting in better reporting of deathbed visions; and the development of various electronic devices has provided new pathways for spirit communications. But the biggest advance in afterlife investigations is the result of the development of hypnosis and the ensuing improvements in regression techniques. Curious minds shall always be grateful for the pioneering work of Colavida and de Rochas, and the contemporary efforts of Bernstein, Goldberg, Netherton, Sutphen, Wambach, and Weiss.

While almost all regression therapists have concentrated on revealing the previous earth-lives of their subjects, Michael Newton, Ph.D., has chosen a different, and apparently more difficult, route that makes him a pioneer among pioneers. Dr. Newton has developed and implemented regression techniques that allow his subjects to remember the time spent *between* lives — the time spent in heaven. From this has sprung a new branch of regression therapy called LBL, for Life-

Between-Lives therapy. Newton has written three books[81] detailing his subjects' experiences. Now semi-retired, he remains devoted to training other therapists to carry on the LBL work.

LBL patients paint remarkably consistent pictures of the afterlife, pictures that neither reflect their religious upbringing nor fulfill their prior expectations. It is difficult to imagine any explanation for this universal agreement except that the memories are what they claim to be — accurate portrayals of a real heaven.

Beyond their inner consistency, we have, of course, no way of confirming the descriptions of lives between lives. One of Newton's cases[82] is worth relating here, however, because it is especially evidential of reincarnation in that it involves two living subjects relating the same story of a past-life incident from two different perspectives.

Maureen and Dale were born near San Francisco, California, almost at the same time; but if they were supposed to live together the fates must have screwed up somehow because they took 50 years to find one another. By then, they were living 3,000 miles apart and had to make their connection in a computer chat room; a room dedicated, appropriately enough, to discussions of life after death. Almost immediately they felt a strong affinity for each other and found that they had an

---

[81] Titles are: *Journey of Souls*, *Destiny of Souls*, and *Life Between Lives: Hypnotherapy for Spiritual Regression*.

[82] Newton *Destiny of Souls* pp. 266-274.

unusual amount in common. Dale had read Dr. Newton's first book and he and Maureen agreed to undergo regression sessions to see if they were friends or lovers in the past.

During Maureen's session, she relived being a woman named Samantha who is getting ready for her 18th birthday party in 1923. She lives near San Francisco, and the party is in a downtown mansion. When she is moved forward to the party, she tells of dancing with her boyfriend Rick and drinking the liquor that he and his friends smuggled into the party. Rick suggests that they need to be alone and so they sneak out of the house by a side entrance and drive away in his red roadster. For awhile, she feels the warm wind in her hair and the joy of being with the man she loves. But the man she loves is paying more attention to the woman he loves than to the road ahead. He is driving too fast and, when they encounter a sharp curve on the Pacific Coast Road, the car goes over a cliff.

When Dale was regressed, he told the same story from Rick's point of view, the only difference being that his soul abandons his body as the roadster falls through the air, whereas Samantha tells of dying in the cold ocean water.

In follow-up discussions, both Dale and Maureen spoke of being strangely uncomfortable driving on certain roads around San Francisco. It is important to note, however, that neither Dale nor Maureen, prior to their sessions, had any idea of being Rick and Samantha or of dying in an auto accident. Dale had only flown out to meet Maureen for the first time in person on the day before they met with Dr. Newton. Each was regressed individually and privately and there was no communication between them in the interim between Maureen's session and Dale's.[83]

End Case 18

"The fact that Dale and Maureen described the same scenes certainly deflates any theories regarding imagination or subconscious memories," I said. "I wonder if there are any surviving police records of the accident?"

"Perhaps one of our readers can find out. Per Samantha's account, the accident occurred on the night of June 26th 1923. (Although, according to Dr. Newton,[84] dates given during regressions are not always reliable, as a subject may supply a date with strong personal significance rather than the date of the day in question.)"

"Well, I like the fact that two people both testify to the same events. But I don't think we can rule out the possibility of collusion between Dale and Maureen prior to the sessions."

"There is no reason to suspect it either, but you are correct, the possibility is there and does weaken the case somewhat.

---

[83] Per personal correspondence with Newton, May 2005.

[84] Personal correspondence, July 2005.

"A small thing that I believe strengthens the case, on the other hand, is that the two souls went their separate ways en route to heaven. If this was a fabrication, or a dream that Maureen somehow telepathically shared with Dale, how could she resist having the two soulmates rise together above the moonlit breakers, astral hand in astral hand?"

"It does make for an enchanting picture."

"Funny you should use that term, for the next case centers around a picture.

"Most of the cases in the hypnotic-regression literature are described by therapists, either directly or via journalists, so this story is special because it is told, and told most convincingly, by the subject himself."

Case 19 – The Policeman and the Painter

Captain Robert L. Snow, Commander of the Homicide Branch of the Indianapolis Police Department, veteran of 30-years on the force, and author of four books on police procedures, thought of himself as a down-to-earth, street-wise, and rational cop. So, when he underwent regression hypnosis — as a result of a colleague's dare — he felt more than a little foolish and a lot like he was wasting his time.

He was astonished, therefore, when, after spending an uncomfortable half-hour on a psychologist's couch, he suddenly found himself standing almost naked on the slope of a mountain. For a brief time, he experienced the life of a primitive man struggling to survive in an ancient forest before dying in a lonely cave.

Soon afterwards, the scene shifted and he was standing before an easel, paintbrush in hand, studying a somewhat hunchbacked woman by gaslight. In briefly living several scenes from this life, Snow discovered that the artist resided in a large city in the late 1800s, spent some time in France, was recognized as a talented portrait painter although he didn't care to paint portraits (he did so only because they paid well), and many other mundane facts. When the hypnosis session was concluded, the image that stuck in Snow's mind most forcefully was of the painting of the hunchbacked woman in a long gown that he had seen, nearly completed, on the artist's easel.

Captain Snow was surprised, to say the least, that he had actually entered a hypnotic trance and experienced several highly realistic creations of his subconscious mind. But that was all that he was willing to admit. Nevertheless, as days passed, he couldn't get his thoughts off of the session. Finally, he decided that the painting he could remember so vividly was the key. If he could prove that he had seen the painting somewhere before in this, his 20th-century-policeman's life, then he might be able to forget about possible past-lives and move on with the present one.

Assuming the task would prove to be simple because the picture must be famous, Snow went to the art section of the city library and commenced to scan the picture books. He failed to find a picture of the painting. In fact, after many months of intense detective work and hundreds of hours spent in art libraries and art galleries, all he found was frustration. So, when his wife suggested that some time off might be useful, he agreed to a short vacation in New Orleans. And there, in a city he had never before visited, off an obscure street in the French Quarter, in the far corner of the front parlor of a small art gallery, Captain Robert L. Snow came suddenly face to face with artist J. Carroll Beckwith's portrait of a slightly hunchbacked woman in a long gown. It was perched there on an easel almost exactly as he had last seen it, some 100 years before. "I stared open-mouthed at the portrait," he later wrote,[85] "reliving an experience I'd had once when I grabbed onto a live wire ... huge voltage surged up and down my arms and legs. ... There was absolutely no doubt at all that this was the portrait I had seen myself painting while under hypnosis." But his no-nonsense side refused to go away; Snow's next thought was: "Now I just had to find a logical explanation for everything."

What he found from the gallery owner was that the painting had been part of a private estate from the time of its creation and was never in the public eye until purchased by the gallery. What he found from several more months of investigation was that Beckwith's career matched the data from the hypnosis sessions in at least 28 particulars and nothing he could find contradicted

---

[85] Snow, pp. 79 & 84.

his impressions except for Mrs. Beckwith's first name (which he had been uncertain of from the first). Most of these facts were preserved only in Beckwith's private journals and had never been published. Finally, even Snow was forced to admit that there really was no "logical explanation" and that, as he said when telling of his visit to Beckwith's grave: "I realized I had nothing to be frightened of ... I knew there couldn't be any ghosts or spirits here because the spirit that had been in Beckwith's body was now in mine."

End Case 19

"Consider the three possible outcomes of Captain Snow's search for the painting," he suggested, as the sky darkened and the wind began to deliver the rain it had promised since breakfast. "First, it could have been displayed or reproduced in a public venue or document. Second, it could not have existed at all except in Snow's imagination. And, third, it could be real but beyond his access. How do you think each possibility would affect the case?"

"If Snow had found that the painting had been reproduced in a time and place where he could have seen it," I said, "he would have assumed that he had simply forgotten that viewing until his subconscious mind offered it up during hypnosis. In which case, he would never have investigated further and found the other 28 correspondences, and there would be no case.

"If Snow had never found the painting, because it didn't exist or had been destroyed or remained in a private collection, he would never have uncovered Beckwith's name, and sooner or later he would have stopped looking. Again, no case."

"It would appear, then," he summarized, "that Snow's rather inexplicable obsession with finding the painting had to be combined with his wife's sudden desire to visit New Orleans and the gallery's recent purchase and prominent display of the painting, or we would have no story. I cannot conceive of all this occurring by chance alone. But if, by some stretch, other people can, the remaining cases are bound to change their minds."

"Before moving on," I said, "there is another thing that strikes me as especially evidential in the Beckwith case. The one piece of evidence that Snow got wrong was Mrs. Beckwith's name, yet that surely would be part of the public record, no matter how scanty that record might be. This is a pretty strong indication that Snow's source was indeed the regression, rather than any prior experience or research."

"Good point," he said, moving to close the windows across the back, where the rain was coming in. "And it brings to mind an interesting footnote to the case. Snow, while in trance and speaking as Beckwith, said that he was in a city and meeting a woman named Amanda. After his book was published, Snow reports,[86] research by a librarian revealed that

---

[86] Per personal correspondence, October, 2005.

the young Beckwith dated a girl named Amanda, who moved to New York City at about the same time Beckwith did. So, it wasn't that Snow got the name of his wife wrong, it was just that he incorrectly assumed that the girl Amanda must be his wife.

"As with so many of these cases, the deeper one looks, the more convincing they become."

I nodded agreement and continued reading.

Case 20 — Death in the Garment District

Dr. Morris Netherton began specializing in what he terms "Past Lives Therapy" around 1970. He does not call what he does "hypnosis" as he relies on word associations rather than the more common types of trance induction, but his methods seem to work well for accessing traumas in past and pre-natal lives. In 1978 he published a collection of his cases that includes several with exceptional verification; one of these is the story of Rita McCullum.[87]

During regression, a patient (whom Netherton does not name) related numerous trials and tribulations of a personality named Rita, who was born in 1903. We shall limit our coverage of Rita's tale to the period beginning in the late 1920s in midtown Manhattan. She and her husband, Keith McCullum, had finally brought their fledgling clothing company to the brink of success. In the winter of 1928, the overwork involved in this accom-

---

[87] Netherton, pp. 166-168.

plishment resulted in Keith contracting pneumonia and dying. Only one year later, Rita's son died of polio. That October, 1929, the stock market crashed and the Great Depression began. Despite her heroic struggles over the next few years, Rita ended up broke and alone and suicidal.

On the 11th of June, 1933, a destitute and despondent Rita McCullum went into the cutting room of her defunct factory, looped a rope over the bars that were used to hold garments, and hung herself.

Such is the tale that was told by a regressed patient in Dr. Netherton's office in the mid-1970s. And such is the tale confirmed by a notarized death certificate that Netherton later obtained from the New York City Hall of Records. The certificate states that one Rita McCullum, age 30 (and thus born in 1903) committed suicide by hanging on 11 June 1933 at an address in the heart of the garment district in Manhattan.

End Case 20

"So what has Netherton been doing since 1978," I asked. "I don't think I've heard of the man."

"That's probably because you're not a psychologist. Netherton has been concentrating on helping patients and on teaching other therapists his techniques. As laymen, we're interested in the sensational evidence he uncovers from time to time, but his focus is on healing ... as it should be.

"The next case, by the way, certainly qualifies as 'sensational.'"

Case 21 — The Numbers of the Beast

During a training demonstration in Brazil, Dr. Netherton regressed a young woman suffering from agoraphobia (the fear of being in open places). Starting when she was 16 years of age, her fears had steadily grown until she was very uncomfortable when not near her home and she trusted only her immediate family.

While regressed, she recalled a life that ended in a German concentration camp. According to her story, when she arrived at the camp, a guard burned an identification number into her arm. As she told of this, she suddenly began screaming and clutching at her arm. Netherton noticed red welts appearing on the woman's arm. These began to resolve themselves into numbers. An elderly psychologist sitting nearby jumped up and rolled up his sleeve to show similar numbers that had been burned into his arm at just such a camp. The man was so excited that it took awhile for Dr. Netherton to calm him down so that the session could continue.

During this session, the recalled personality gave numerous facts identifying herself, her family, and the camp. She said that she died after suffering through several months of exposure to the harsh elements there.

The numbers on the subject's arm faded away when the session ended. But, an assistant at the demonstration had taken a photograph of the numbers and an inquiry was made by sending only that identification number to the Holocaust Museum in Israel. The report sent back by the museum described a young girl whose name, birth date, parent's name, village of birth, and date of death perfectly matched the facts given by the subject.

According to Dr. Netherton,[88] "These facts are unimportant when compared to the effectiveness of the session. It changed the young lady's feelings, and she began returning to her normal life."

End Case 21

"As evidence of reincarnation, the facts cited here are anything but unimportant," I said, looking up from the manual.

"Yes, but the therapeutic affect of the session does add validity. What do you think of the appearance of the numbers?"

"A little difficult to take," I admitted.

"But very difficult to fake," he pointed out. "If the female subject were a skilled illusionist and well-practiced at feigning trance, I suppose fraud would be possible. But I can imagine no motivation for achieving such a deception and then not claiming credit for it. In actuality, the woman did not appreciate her sudden notoriety and, for awhile, Nether-

---

[88] Netherton, Morris, *The Psychology of Past-life Regression*, web page: http://www.centrodifusao.hpg.ig.com.br/morris.htm. Additional information per personal conversation with Dr. Netherton, August 2005.

ton even changed the reported locale of the incident from Brazil to the Netherlands in an effort to give her some respite from the curious."

"Well then, it must be accepted as solid evidence," I said, "but I do prefer less sensational episodes that involve more than one testimony."

"We can handle that," he replied. "I believe you'll find the next case to be unique."

Case 22 – The Apprentice Murderer

Dr. Bruce Goldberg has regressed literally thousands of patients in his 30-year career in hypnotherapy. Most all of his cases are interesting and evidential, but two of them, when combined one with the other, offer both a fascinating story and a unique proof of Survival and reincarnation.

The first case concerns a patient, a retail clerk, who complained of always being dominated and manipulated by co-workers, customers, and even relatives. Several age-regressions were tried, revealing a childhood of being pushed around by most everyone, but no clear initiating incident. Then past-life regressions were attempted and, after four rather unproductive sessions, the man began to speak as a fellow named Thayer, living in Bavaria in the year 1132.

In the opening scene of this regression, Thayer was eating supper *under* the table. He explained this bizarre situation by saying that he was apprenticed to a goldsmith named Gustave who often beat him, sodomized him, and kept him chained to the table whenever the shop was closed. And, when the shop was open for business, Gustave would humiliate Thayer in front of the customers, especially when Clotilde, a nice girl from a wealthy family, came in to purchase something.

Moved forward to a significant moment in his life, Thayer told a dreadful tale of getting into a fight with his master, being stabbed in the stomach with a metal-working tool, and looking down on his own dead body.

Mainly as a result of reliving these ancient events, Dr. Goldberg's patient rapidly gained self-esteem and confidence and went on to pull his life together. [It is an accepted principle of hypnotherapy that getting such past-life incidents into the awareness of the current mind has the effect of eliminating or greatly reducing their debilitating effects. Why this should be true is unclear.]

About 18 months later, Goldberg was working with another patient, an attorney, whose major complaint was that he felt overwhelmed by urges to manipulate and dominate people. It seems his guilty conscious was causing insomnia and eating disorders. As with the above case, normal hypnotic suggestions and age-regressions met with only limited success. As you have probably already surmised, past-life regression revealed that this man had been a master goldsmith named Gustave in early 12th-century Bavaria. He complained about his incompetent apprentice and, when asked for the fellow's name, said it was Thayer. "At this point,"

Goldberg reports, "my skin began to crawl. However, my obligation was to my current patient, and it was important to continue this regression as if nothing unusual had happened."[89]

Without any coaching from Goldberg, Gustave proceeded to say that he enjoyed beating his apprentice, that a certain girl named Clotilde was a distraction to the boy, and many other facts that exactly complemented the story that "Thayer" had told while reclining on the same couch over a year earlier. The culmination, too, was identical in all pertinent particulars: Gustave told of his apprentice resisting attempts to chain him to the table, getting into a fight, and then killing the boy by stabbing him in the stomach.

Of course, Goldberg never breached his patients' confidence by telling either about the other, so, unless they happened to recognize themselves in Goldberg's book or this one, neither man currently is aware that his nemesis of the past is his neighbor today.

End Case 22

"That's a really impressive story," I said. "The number of specific details (including unusual names and uncommon activities) given by both subjects certainly rules out any idea of coincidence or lucky guesses. The fact that these details are part of a time and place alien to the patients makes it even more convincing. Altogether, this is one of the most evidential cases I have yet seen. I'm

---

[89] Goldberg, pp. 112-125.

not certain, however, why you referred to it as 'unique'?"

"As far as I am aware," he replied, "this is the only case in anyone's files in which two hypnotic subjects describe the same incidents without either knowing of the other's existence."

"Can we be certain of that? Could it be a hoax?"

"Any suggestion of trickery is fatuous for several reasons: the effort and skill needed to fool a seasoned hypnotherapist twice would be monumental, there was no reason to wait several sessions to begin their fabrications, the time delay between the two appearances is overly long, and the subjects have gained neither notoriety nor money from their efforts. In fact, the sessions would have been rather costly to them.

"I agree with you that the story of Thayer and Gustave is one of the strongest proofs of reincarnation, that is why I saved it until the end ... or almost the end," he said, and nodded one last time towards the book in my lap.

Case 23 – A Town Reborn

Those who teach reincarnation often speak of souls traveling in packs. Your spouse today might have been your best friend in some yesterday, your current neighbor could be a teacher in a past life, and so on. These configurations are intentional, having been carefully planned by the souls involved during their time between lives. A subject undergoing hypnotic regression may say that so-and-so in their current life is the reincarnation of some principal person in their past life, but such claims almost always lack supportive testimony. This is because friends and relatives typically are not invited to observe the sessions.

There are exceptions to every rule, however, and one such uncommon observance led to what is probably the best corroborated collection of past lives ever revealed. Marge Rieder, Ph.D., practices hypnotherapy in the town of Lake Elsinore, California. She had a patient named Maureen, who was reliving a past life as a woman in Virginia during the American Civil War. Maureen invited a friend named Barbara to attend one of the sessions and Dr. Rieder, who was also a friend of Barbara, allowed her to observe. Midway through the session, Barbara passed a note to the therapist that said: "Ask her if I was there." Rieder reports that she was shocked to hear Maureen say that Barbara was her mother-in-law in that life.

To make a complex and fascinating story overly simple, the long-term results of that one hypnosis session led Rieder to become the only hypnotherapist known to have uncovered almost an entire town full of people reincarnated together. During a 17-year investigation, one subject after another named others who currently lived in the vicinity of Lake Elsinore but who had also lived in the little town of Millboro, Virginia in the mid 19th century. So far, more than 50 people have remembered lives in that time and place, although only three had visited the state of Virginia in their current lives and none had ever heard of Millboro. At least, they hadn't heard of it until Rieder's first book[90] was published. Afterwards, several people contacted Rieder and asked to be hypnotized because they were certain that they, too, were part of the story. Remarkably, hypnosis often revealed that such convictions were merely wishful thinking; they actually could recall no lives as "Millboreans."

The name of the town itself provides significant support to the case, as it was pronounced "Marlboro" by most of the regressed. The reality of the town at first seemed doubtful when no "Marlboro" could be found on maps of Virginia. But when one entranced subject was induced to write down the name, she wrote "Millboro." There was a town named Millboro on the map and it appeared to fit the descriptions perfectly. Upon investigation, Rieder discovered that many residents of the area around Millboro pronounce the name as "Marlboro" to this day.[91]

A majority of the subjects who are part of the group had not met when they first underwent hypnosis, yet they have all told consistent stories and described the same locations, without any overlap of personalities. Most evidential, are the buried rooms and tunnels that several subjects described as being utilized by the underground

---

[90] Rieder has written three books on the subject: *Mission to Millboro*, *Return to Millboro*, and *Millboro and More*.

[91] Rieder, *Mission to Millboro*, p. xvii.

railway in aiding slaves and orphaned Union soldiers to travel north. Although no resident in the current town of Millboro was aware of these, and they were not described in any document nor located on any known map, excavations revealed them to exist precisely as described by Rieder's entranced subjects in California — right down to the uncommon color of the walls.

End Case 23

"I was especially impressed with the fact that some people undergoing regression fully expected to relive a life in Millboro, but failed to do so."

"Yes," he agreed, "it goes to show that preconceptions have nothing to do with the results.

"Another interesting twist is that Rieder had another hypnotist regress her subjects, but the results were the same."

"Well, if I wasn't already convinced of an afterlife, I sure would be now.

"But we have yet to address the problem of distinguishing actual past lives of the current subjects from memories being telepathically received from discarnate souls."

"Okay. Here are my top ten reasons for believing in the reincarnation hypothesis," he said, handing me a typewritten sheet of paper. While I read, he busied himself preparing a snack of sliced apples and cheese.

The Top Ten Reasons
For Reincarnation Not Being an Illusion
Caused by Discarnate Spirits

10. If there is no reincarnation, then the evidence we have of past lives would have to be the result of thousands of discarnate spirits deceitfully projecting their memories into the minds of hypnotized humans. It is unlikely that there could be so many souls both able and willing to commit such fraud.

9. Since humans may elect to undergo past-life regression at any time, a fiction of reincarnation could only be maintained if each human had a discarnate soul assigned to hang around just in case. And being available just once isn't enough, for most therapies access the same life numerous times. Actually, each human would require several souls in constant attendance, as most regressions uncover more than one past-life.

8. The difficulties raised in number 9 are vastly increased with group reincarnations. For example, are we to believe that the soul of Samantha managed to transfer its memories into the mind of Maureen while the soul of Rick hung around waiting for the opportunity to try and transfer his memories into the mind of Dale? When we consider the 50 some souls involved in the Millboro case, the idea becomes transparently ludicrous.

7. Then there is the question of motivation. Why would a soul want its personal memories to

be claimed by someone else? Such a transference goes against everything we know about the psychology of personal identity. As has been demonstrated over and over again during mediumistic communications, souls adamantly want to be known as themselves.

6. Our understanding of mental telepathy is stretched close to, and perhaps beyond, the breaking point by the idea of communicating memories of subjective experiences -- the feeling of being in love, the intention to accomplish a goal, etc. -- that are so often part of the regression scene.

5. In hypnotic regressions using relatively light trances, both men and women recall past lives as males more often than lives as females. This makes sense when you consider that the lives of males tend, on average, to be more dramatic (more competitive, more daring, more active, etc.) than female lives, and that lives with more drama are more easily remembered. On the other hand, deeper trances tend to access lives without regard to their intensity, including the truly boring ones, as in:

> "What are you doing now?" "Weaving baskets."

> "Okay, go forward five years. What are you doing now?" "Weaving baskets."

> "Okay, go forward ten years. What are you doing now?" "Teaching my granddaughter to weave baskets."

And deeper trances reveal an equal number of male and female lives.[92] There is no known reason for such correlates to arise if the life stories were being dictated by discarnate souls.

4. Additional regressions may reveal additional past-lives, but the original cast always remains. Subjects never claim to be Napoleon one week and Nelson the next. This makes perfect sense if reincarnation is valid, and no sense if the regressions rely on the whims of discarnate souls and the vagaries of telepathy.

3. Regressions reveal only one personality per era. If a subject recalls several lives, they will occur before or after one another, virtually never simultaneously.[93] Telepathically "remembering" the lives of some other souls would not be likely to result in the same degree of exclusivity.

2. A whole bunch of psychiatrists, psychologists, and other trained hypnotherapists have confirmed for themselves that past-life regressions and LBL regressions are almost always therapeutic. We have no reason to think that remembering someone else's memories would likewise be so effective in alleviating symptoms.

1. And the number one reason that reincarnation is not a deception of discarnate spirits is that the spirits say so! For awhile, many Spiritualists scorned the idea of reincarnation. But

---

[92] TenDam, p.188.

[93] Claims have been made that, in rare circumstances, a soul will divide its essence among two physical bodies simultaneously. See TenDam, p. 321 and Newton, *Destiny of Souls*, p. 116.

then, several of those who were against the idea in life became ardent supporters in their post-mortem communications via mediums. Today, you would be hard pressed to find an astral entity who does not affirm the reality of reincarnation.

After studying these reasons briefly, I handed the sheet back to him and he tucked it into my copy of the *Casebook*, saying that I would need it later.

"Are you convinced that reincarnation is the most reasonable and likely explanation for the phenomena?" he asked.

"I am so convinced."

"Then have some apple and let us return to our exploration of heaven."

The remainder of the morning was essentially a Q and A session. My questions were neither as cogent nor as well organized as they appear here, but I felt that a bit of editing would make for easier reading.

Sunday Morning III

Celestial Q & A

If we harden our hearts against dogmatism in some quarters, sentimentalism in others, and wishful-thinking in ourselves; if we carefully scrutinize the evidence (especially the odder and more unexpected items); if we try to develop a reasonable theory of what is likely to be going on, and check it wherever possible against any relevant facts obtainable, I believe we shall gradually form a pretty clear conception of what post-mortem conditions are like, and why.

— Whately Carington[94]

Q. What does it feel like to die? Does it hurt?

A. The cause of death might be painful briefly, although the soul will often abandon the body to avoid excessive suffering. One of the best descriptions I've read was received in 1917 via automatic writing from a recently passed soldier named Thomas Dowding:

---

[94] Carington p. 12.

I had been struck by a shell splinter. There was no pain. The life was knocked out of my body; again, I say, there was no pain. Then I found that the whole of myself — all, that is, that thinks and sees and feels and knows — was still alive and conscious! I had begun a new chapter of life. I will tell you what I felt like. It was as if I had been running hard until, hot and breathless, I had thrown my overcoat away. The coat was my body, and if I had not thrown it away I should have been suffocated.[95]

According to Doctor Helen Wambach, 90-percent of her regression subjects recalled their death (at the end of a past life) as being a pleasant experience.[96]

Q. What's the first thing that will happen when I die?

A. If your death is presaged by illness or debilitation, you may be aware of visits by the spirits of deceased loved ones for a week or so prior to dying. Your initial experiences after biological death will likely be similar to what NDErs report. You will find your 'self' hovering above your physical body. It may take a while to realize you have died. You will be free of pain and feel great. You may hang around for a little while, perhaps as long as a few days, watching your funeral arrangements and trying to communicate with those you are leaving behind. Such efforts will be generally unsuccessful. Or, you may elect to move

---

[95] Pole, p. 16.

[96] Wambach, p. 63.

on immediately. Then a sense of rapid travel, perhaps through a tunnel or up a stairway, at the end of which you will experience a sensation of being approached by and then enveloped by a brilliant light that exudes reassuring love and compassion. From this point on, you will receive whatever assistance and guidance you require. If you are completing one of your first lifetimes on earth, you will be met by a compassionate spirit who will guide you back home. If you are an old hand at dying, you may feel confident finding your own way.

Those who adamantly believe that bodily death equals absolute extinction of consciousness can block these inputs so effectively that they do, indeed, undergo temporary oblivion. But no soul is ever abandoned forever to its own devices.

Other souls may believe in an afterlife yet still require special attention to make the transition. The guides are skilled in gaining a soul's trust and getting it to understand the truth of what has happened and what the next steps will be like. I know of no better example of this than the one Seth relates concerning the time he was a spirit guide to a man who was conflicted between the power of Allah and the power of Moses. "He was a very likable guy," Seth reports[97] "and under the circumstances I did not mind when he seemed to expect a battle for his soul. ... A friend and I, with some others, staged the ceremony, and from opposite clouds in the sky Allah and I [acting

---

[97] Roberts, *Seth Speaks* pp. 141-142

the part of Moses] shouted out our claims upon his soul — while he, poor man, cowered on the ground between us. ... Finally the opposing clouds in which we appeared came closer. In my hand I held a tablet that said 'Thou shalt not kill.' Allah held a sword. As we came closer we exchanged these items, and our followers merged. We came together, forming the image of a sun, and we said: 'We are one.' The two diametrically opposed ideas had to merge or the man would have had no peace, and only when these opposites were united could we begin to explain his situation."

Other souls that require special care are those who have been focused for so long on their various ailments that they project those ill conditions upon their ethereal body. The guides sometimes must "treat" these astral ailments before they can get their new "patient" to comprehend his or her heavenly situation.

And, to further complicate matters, there are those who die in their sleep and think that the death experience is all just a dream. It sometimes takes the guides quite a while to convince them that they are, indeed, dead.

Q. **Why would some souls have been on Earth more than others?**

A. The Source expresses Itself in many dimensions, some are physical like Earth, others are not. Thus, prior to coming to Earth, a soul may have spent several millennia incarnating on other planets or as a spirit in other realms. Our Earth, by the way, is one of the more recently opened venues; which is one reason it is currently such a popular destination.[98]

Also, new souls are still being created. Thus, some souls are older than our physical universe, others were born this morning.

Q. **Sounds like souls have a life cycle. Do souls grow old and die?**

A. To me, it seems right and reasonable that (as many theologies teach) souls ultimately return to the Source from which they came (in as much as they ever really left). But we have no way of knowing what happens at such levels.

I should point out here that Survival and immortality are not necessarily the same thing. We might live many lives and then simply cease to reincarnate. We might enjoy heaven for ten thousand years and then go "poof." Even the wisest spirit guide has no way of knowing. So we're really just speculating when we speak of ultimate destinations.

Q. **When souls incarnate on other physical planets besides Earth, do they reside in human or human-like bodies? For that matter, can we come back as animals or insects?**

A. At this time, no one seems to have gathered much information on the type of bodies a soul might inhabit elsewhere. One explanation for this lack is

---

[98] Homewood, p. 76.

that the images are blocked because we would find them too creepy or repulsive. A more probable — and palatable — reason is simply that no soul who has spent any amount of time incarnated on another planet and then come to Earth has yet undergone a regression extensive enough to reveal such information.

As far as souls inhabiting animals, the short answer is "no." To understand the full answer you must understand that souls created the universe. It was souls that created matter, and stars, and planets. It was souls that created bugs and trees and chimpanzees. This is not blasphemy because <u>souls are parts of the Source</u> (call it God, Allah, Creator, All That Is, or whatever name you wish). Souls are the mechanisms that the Source uses to express Itself. In the process of doing all this creating and expressing — which occupied untold eons and was certainly performed according to the laws of nature — individual souls often semi-merged with their creations for brief periods. I use the prefix 'semi' because bugs and trees and chimpanzees are not suitable for containing more than a small bit of a soul for a brief time. Who hasn't wondered what it would be like to be an eagle or a lion? Well, the souls had the opportunity to find out, so they did. And that is why memories of past lives sometimes include sensations of being an animal or, in very rare cases, the feeling of being a plant.[99]

---

[99] Knight, *Ramtha*, pp. 82-87, and Newton, *Journey of Souls*, p. 168.

Q. **Were humans created in the same way?**

A. Yes. After many millennia of creative play with millions of solar systems and billions of life forms, some souls decided to create an animal suitable for housing a major portion of a soul for an indefinite period. Tired of temporary excursions, they wanted to experience what it was really like to live fully immersed in a physical body. So they modified an existing animal (giving it a larger brain, different hormonal structure, etc.) and merged with the result.

They soon discovered, however, that the pretense of being a human (or a Klingon or whatever) was tough to maintain, especially in the face of pain or immediate threat to life. Every time a cave bear took a swipe at a man, the inhabiting soul would pop out in fright, leaving the man rather disoriented. (A lot of cave folks were lost that way.) The souls' solution was to hide their memories and sense of 'soulness' deep in their unconscious mind when they entered a biological body. This conditional amnesia also allowed for a fresh approach to life's challenges.

As time went on, this 'incarnation game' became one of the most popular pastimes throughout the universe.

Only in the past century (a mere moment to the Source) have humans of our era developed reliable techniques to temporarily overcome our self-imposed amnesia and access the soul's hidden memories of itself.

Q. Are there other reasons that recall of our past lives is repressed?

A. Yes, several.

For an actor to convincingly play a character on stage, he must focus fully on that role. If you were playing the role of Romeo, your performance would be seriously degraded if you let your mind wander to the list of items that your wife asked you to pick up from the all-night grocery on your way home. Imagine how much greater a problem if you attempted to play Romeo while rehearsing in your head your lines from *Hamlet*!

There may be times when knowledge of a past-life event can benefit us in this life, but full and constant awareness of another life would seriously interfere with the living of this one. There will be plenty of opportunity between lives to compare and contrast our previous incarnations. It's best to focus on the present, and be happy that we're not asked to live more than one life at a time.

Another reason becomes apparent when we consider the immense frustration that would be faced by a fully conscious adult trapped within an immobile and generally incapable infant body for several years.

There could be other reasons as well. For example, if we knew what awaited us, we might be too ready to leave when things started getting tough on this side.

I am particularly fond of a rationale offered by Rudyard Kipling as he tells of a young man whose recall of his past lives fades rapidly when he meets his first love in this life. Musing about the impact on the reproduction of our species if people could remember their very first loves from their very first lives, Kipling wrote: "Now I understand why the Lords of Life and Death shut the doors so carefully behind us. It is that we may not remember our first wooings. Were it not so, our world would be without inhabitants in a hundred years."[100]

Despite all these impediments, sometimes people *do* recall part of a past life, even without being hypnotized. Dr. Ian Stevenson has dedicated his career to studying such occurrences.

Q. **Just how sure are you that such accounts and explanations are accurate?**

A. Discarnate entities generally do not use words to communicate. What information comes to us must be processed and translated into terms we can understand. All information-processing involves some distortion, so no single source should be relied on absolutely. Most points I am making here are synthesized from many sources and, while there might be some discrepancies in the details, they can generally be relied on as facts supported by the available evidence.

---

[100] Kipling, Rudyard, "The Finest Story in the World," in *Many Inventions*, 1893.

Q. Do you think that souls might still enter animals for short periods?

A. I really have no evidence that they do, but that might explain the occasional heroic acts of some pets.

Q. You mean Lassie is inspired by angels?

A. Could be.

Q. What are angels?

A. At times, a soul in spirit can get the opportunity to assist a soul in flesh, and so be perceived as angelic. But angels are not a special class of beings. In fact, there are no 'classes' of beings. There ain't nobody here but us souls. Some souls are old, others are young; some are advanced, others are novices; some have incarnated, others have not; all are of equal value to God.[101]

Q. Who are the guides you speak of?

A. They are souls who stand ready to lend assistance and aid to recent arrivals in heaven. They may be taking time-out from their other heavenly duties to accomplish this or they may be still among the physically living and be doing a little dream work.[102]

Q. Where is heaven?

A. There is only one universe and, whether it twinkles or sprinkles (as we speculated last night) or does something else altogether, all its planes or dimensions or what-have-you co-exist in the same place.

---

[101] Crenshaw, p. 45.

[102] Roberts, *Seth Speaks*, p. 135.

Thus, no matter where you are, heaven is right there and right here.

Q. **So, what is heaven like?**

A. There are many planes of existence. The one we are referring to as "heaven" is the plane where most souls find themselves immediately after completing a life on Earth.

One of the points on which there is strong agreement is that much of heaven simply cannot be described in physical terms. Thus, our picture is somewhat confused and certainly incomplete. In general, though, we can assume a few characteristics.

First impressions of the world beyond are highly individualized. Some see colorful fields of flowers, some rainbow-filled skyscapes, others shining crystal cities. Upon deeper exploration, however, a more uniform picture emerges. Almost everyone speaks of having to traverse a haze or misty area before entering heaven itself.

Overall, heaven appears essentially as a structure of light. Imagine that all the stars in the night sky were bright enough to be seen in the daytime. The background sky would be a field of light against which can be seen a vast sea of brighter lights, and clusters of lights, and misty clouds of lights. Most sense that heaven is exceedingly immense, but not necessarily infinite. Some detect a curvature that suggests a spherical shape.

In your immediate vicinity, heaven will appear pretty much as you want or need it to appear. The picture painted by the movie *What Dreams May Come* is fairly accurate in this regard.

Most sources agree that heaven is not ephemeral, indistinct, or somber. Indeed, it is reported to seem solidly real to its inhabitants. Also, because our human proclivities for power, prestige, and profit don't necessarily die with our bodies, heaven is not always harmonious.

Q. **You mentioned going "home." Does my soul reside in a particular place in heaven?**

A. The home I referred to is more a group of souls than a precise location. This group, or cluster, consists of souls you have lived with, reincarnated with, loved and known intimately ever since you were created. Once you are with them again and regain full memory of who they are, you will know how it truly feels to be home.

Q. **But what if the other souls in my group are all currently incarnated? Will there be no one to greet me?**

A. There are three reasons why there will always be someone home to greet you. First, each group has guides and teachers who are no longer incarnating. Second, souls can and do travel about while their physical body sleeps, so they can attend your 'Welcome Back' party. And third, the entirety of a soul never incarnates; there is always a significant portion remaining in heaven, although rather dormant. So you will not only be rejoining yourself, but all of the others will be there, at least partially, to greet you.[103]

Q. **Is my contact with other souls limited to those in my cluster?**

A. Not at all. Many of your activities, both purposeful and recreational, will involve souls beyond your group. Souls can locate and converse with one another as they wish.[104]

Q. **Most people have more than one love during their life; many have more than one spouse, and they all don't necessarily like one another. Getting them all back together doesn't sound very heavenly.**

A. The people in a cluster do not generally plan lives with such multiple intimacies. Chances are that sequential spouses hale from a variety of heavenly backgrounds. But if such a situation should occur — say, two souls who were brothers are working on envy issues and incarnate as wives of the same man — the earthly grievances won't be carried over to the spirit world. Be assured that it will work out, and it won't be uncomfortable if you're together again.

Sometimes a person without good rapport with their mate will find a wife or husband from a previous life waiting for them in heaven.

---

[103] Newton, *Journey of Souls*, pp. 85 & 155, also Roberts, *Seth Speaks*, p. 354.

[104] Garland, *The Mystery of the Buried Crosses*, p. 181.

Q. Will I receive a new body in heaven?

A. You already are inhabiting the body you will have in heaven, your flesh is currently embedded within this body. In fact, your physical body receives its vitality and strength from this astral body. When you leave behind the physical body, therefore, your astral body will seem quite familiar and real to you.[105] The only time you receive a new body is when you move in the opposite direction — from a higher level/frequency to a lower one.

Q. What will I look like in heaven?

A. The unadorned soul appears as a compact cloud of light. It can be sculpted to any desired semblance. Once acclimated to being again in heaven, you likely will assume the appearance of the last time that you felt good; later you will morph into the age that you felt best. Handicaps and deformities need not be carried over into the spirit world.[106] As time passes, you will probably settle on the look and personality you had in whatever past life pleased you most. Any of these projected images may be modified to fit particular occasions. For instance, if the person who was your son in your most immediate past life dies, you likely will take on the appearance of his parent while welcoming him to the afterlife.

Another factor that can influence the way you look, is the particular job you have taken on in

---

[105] Roberts, *The Seth Material*, p. 143.

[106] Moody, *The Light Beyond*, p. 86.

heaven. For example, if you are escorting a newly deceased Christian, you might assume the guise of Jesus (however your charge thinks Jesus should look) or of an angel, complete with robes and golden wings, or even "take the form of an individual's dearly beloved dead pet"[107] ... Whatever image offers the most comfort.

Q. **How will death change me?**

A. When you die, you will gain a better perspective on who you truly are, but do not expect instant enlightenment. You will not suddenly be a nicer person nor a wiser one. You will not be privy to the arcane secrets of the Knights Templar or the true purpose of the Oak Island earthworks. You will not abruptly comprehend the calculus and your access to the Mind of God will not be noticeably greater than it is now.

The major immediate change will be a lack of the physical urges, needs, and addictions of a biological body; although whatever changes your body has wrought on your psyche may linger for some time.

You will see other souls as they truly are (which is great) and others will see you as you truly are (which might not be so great).

Q. **Will I be judged on how I lived my just-completed life?**

A. Others may guide you but only you will judge yourself. You will have several opportunities to review

---

[107] Roberts, *Seth Speaks*, p. 143.

your just-completed physical life. You will not only see your life from your perspective, but you will experience yourself as others knew you. You will have the joy of experiencing all of the pleasure you have given to others and you will relive all of the pain you caused others to feel. Whether you think of this process as heavenly or hellish will depend very much on the kind of life you led. Be warned: The physical body has a dampening effect on emotions; as a spirit you will feel the emotions of others even more intensely.[108]

You will not give yourself demerits because you were sharing a residence with an animal brain driven by natural needs and drives. "Beastly" lusts that you may now consider shameful are of no concern to anyone in heaven. On the other hand, you *will* have regrets about those times you were unable to control that animal brain and actually injured someone.

Q. **Is there no hell?**

A. Sometimes souls who believe that they have behaved poorly will resist leaving the physical world for fear of being punished in the hereafter; so they hang around in a gloomy haze, often haunting their old habitats. Or, they may create a private environ of fire and brimstone and live in it for awhile. The irony is that by doing so they have condemned themselves to the closest thing to hell there is.

---

[108] Moody, *Reunions*, p.145, and Knight, *Ramtha*, p. 55.

On the other hand, a strong belief in an idyllic heaven wherein angelic souls float around with nothing to do but strum their harps can also be an impediment to progress.[109]

Q. Then evil is not punished?

A. The topic of good and evil is a bit outside the scope of this weekend, so I think I will just repeat two statements, one from the entity Seth: "evil is simply ignorance,"[110] and the other from the entity Ramtha: "the Father sees no wrong; he sees only himself."[111]

And, I might add, "punishment" is just another word for "vengeance" and it is equally ineffective.

Q. Would you let criminals go free?

A. Let's just say that, as a biological being, you have a right (actually, an imperative) to defend yourself as necessary. If this requires isolating criminals from society, so be it. But the idea of hurting another person as some sort of payment for their actions is not in tune with universal principles.

Q. Is the afterlife different for suicides?

A. Those who take their own lives, once they realize that they are still 'alive,' are especially prone to fear what might come next. This is partially the fault of religions that talk of eternal punishment for mortal sins, but there *is* some reason for concern because suicides generally find that killing themselves

---

[109] Roberts, *Seth Speaks*, p. 179.

[110] Roberts, *Seth Speaks*, p. 182.

[111] Knight, *Ramtha*, p. 317, also see p. 124.

changes nothing. They generally end up going through similar ordeals again and again until they achieve the strength to overcome the problem. (This principle does not seem to apply to intentionally ending a life of incurable pain or incapacitation.[112])

Q. **Do you accept the doctrine of karma?**

A. From the time I was about 9 years old until my late teens, I would spend most summer days at a local swimming pool and, when I wasn't splashing around, I was laid out with only a towel to protect me from the hard concrete and only an occasional smear of baby oil ('SPF' was then unknown) to 'protect' my skin from the burning sun. Many years later, the chromosomal damage caused by that intense light, so my doctor says, has resulted in several cancerous lesions on my shoulders.

Karma, I believe, is very much like that. Karma is simply the principle that actions naturally lead to consequences. It has nothing to do with justice. No one is keeping a tally of your sins in one life and meting out punishment in the next. Karma means that your actions affect your character and your character affects your intent for a future life and the decisions you make while living it. Some souls may feel the need to experience the consequences of their actions, but this is always an individual decision.

There are no divine laws mandating punishment, retribution, or compensation for actions in our past lives.

---

[112] Newton, *Journey of Souls*, p.58.

Q. Will I see God?

A. Of course.

Whether you recognize Him or not is another matter. As Seth has spoken: [God's] "energy is so unbelievable that it does indeed form all universes; and because Its energy is within and behind all universes, systems, and fields, It is indeed aware of each sparrow that falls, for It *is* each sparrow that falls."[113] God is what you see wherever you look, here and now or in your future heaven.

Q. Let me rephrase and try again: Will I find myself in the presence of, and directly aware of, that core part of God that remains undivided — that central node in the network of creation?

A. No creditable source has reported any such experience.

Q. What will I do in heaven?

A. Many different things, including resting, playing, learning, and loving. Initially, you'll probably spend some time becoming accustomed to operating in a new environment that has different and less-limiting laws. One important task will be thoroughly reviewing your actions in your past life and analyzing what other choices you might have made. It seems that most souls don't become aware of their other existences until after this review is completed.[114] Another

---

[113] Roberts, *The Seth Material*, pp. 237-238.

[114] Roberts, *Seth Speaks*, p. 138.

major activity for many of us will be the planning of our next life in physical reality.

Q. **Will my memory improve? I'd love to better remember certain scenes from my youth.**

A. We are repeatedly told that nothing is ever lost. I must assume that this means that any event that was ever noticed by a soul can be recovered. So the memories you seek will be available. On the other hand, I doubt it would be possible to 'remember' something you were never aware of, such as the number of red blood cells that passed through your upper lip between 10 and 11 a.m. on Friday the 13th of May, 2005. But, I can't say for sure.

Q. **To what extent is our next life planned**?

A. The evidence shows that no life plan is specified completely. The plan presents the patterns; we fill in the details as we live out our biological lives. Free will always trumps destiny. The decisions of others can change your options (but never without your acquiescence at some level).

Q. **How will I choose my next body/life?**

A. Many things can influence your choice. The strongest determinant generally is the role you will play within your group of souls reincarnating in the same era. Otherwise, a particular interest or talent may be the deciding factor; a person who wishes to develop as a musician or mathematician, for example, might choose parents that are likely to encourage such pursuits. Or, one could select a body with a particular handicap or ability that will provide others with desired opportunities to develop.

Overall, there does appear to be a system of precedence that allows souls with past involvements and entanglements to fulfill commitments and pursue existing objectives. Exactly how such a system is supervised is unclear.

Q. **Many books speak of teachers and students. Is heaven a school?**

A. Numerous entranced people speak of classes and learning as a major activity in the afterlife, but they also insist that souls are never forced to do anything and always have choices. I believe the references to classes stem from our natural desire to learn and to express ourselves, so I wouldn't worry about an eternity of class work.

Perhaps a quote from *Conversations with God* would be relevant here: "School is a place you go if there is something you do not know that you want to know. It is not a place you go if you already know a thing and simply want to <u>experience your know-ingness</u>."[115]

Q. **I thought physical incarnations were the place for learning. What sort of lessons take place in heaven?**

A. Creation is a major subject, for the construction of the multiverse and its biological inhabitants is an on-

---

[115] Walsch, p. 21. Emphasis added.

going process. Then there is training to be escorts, teachers, guides, and other specialities.[116]

Q. Does the 'loving' you mentioned have a sexual component?

A. Souls themselves have no gender, but they can play any role they wish.

Several sources report that spirit lovers can merge their energies in a way that is both blissful and erotic — but not procreative. This supposedly makes Earthly sex pale by comparison. The "Invisibles" put it firmly and succinctly back in the 1930s: "You may rest assured that the beauty of physical mating is not lost, but intensively increased in the spiritual realm."[117]

Q. How long will I stay in heaven before returning to Earth?

A. There is no absolute time schedule. Essentially you return, *if* you return, when you believe you are rested and ready. On average, this will take a few decades. Some rush their return because of obsessive attachments to the physical plane, others return quickly due to feelings that an unfinished job needs immediate attention. A soul can also wait too long. The ties to physical life can weaken after three centuries or so

---

[116] Newton provides a provocative list of such specialities on page 322 of *Destiny of Souls*.

[117] White, *Across the Unknown*, p. 82. Also see: Homewood, p. 101; Miller, pp. 158-166; Monroe, *Journeys Out of the Body*, pp. 193-196; and Newton, *Destiny of Souls*, p. 49.

(Earth time) and re-orientation can become difficult.[118]

Q. **Are most heavenly activities focused on past and future incarnations?**

A. Reading the materials available here on Earth, it would be easy to get that impression, but it is clearly incorrect. Physical incarnations are just one of many pursuits taken up by souls. Many, perhaps most, souls may never occupy a human body. And those that do join the human race do so only temporarily. We have no clue what careers they commence once their biological forays are finished.

Q. **How many lives does each soul live on Earth?**

A. At this moment in history, many souls have not embedded themselves in a human body and may never do so (although "never" is a very long time), some others appear intent on incarnating here indefinitely. Generally, souls that play the biological game here will do so for at least three lives and not more than a hundred or so; the mode being around 30.

Q. **Incarnating on Earth can be a pretty tough gig, and pretty risky too, considering all the opportunities to backslide. Is there some advantage to our physical life here that makes the excursion worthwhile?**

A. Earth lives can be relatively more intense and challenging than time spent on other planes, but I would-

---

[118] Roberts, *Seth Speaks*, p. 171.

n't say "tough" or "risky." Basically people incarnate here because they find the experience fun, pleasurable, or otherwise rewarding. I think the most likely motivations souls have for coming to Earth are that their friends are here and they haven't yet become bored with the place. Some souls apparently believe that they have a duty to "progress" in some fashion, but to whom that duty is owed is not very clear.

Q. **How would a soul's progress be measured?**

A. By its demonstration of wisdom, compassion, willpower, independence, and joy.

Q. **Many spiritualists posit several levels of heaven — the astral, the causal, the mental, etc. Must all souls pass through these as do students through elementary, middle, high school, and college?**

A. Let us say that your home was on a mountain top and you left to go exploring. You traveled down the mountain slope, penetrated the encircling jungle, crossed a desert, sailed an ocean, traversed a great forest, and ended up visiting a little house on the prairie. When you decided to return to your aerie there would be many paths to take you home, but all would require first leaving the prairie, going back through the forest, re-crossing the ocean, the desert, and the jungle, and climbing back up the mountain. So it is with souls, who first left the Source as pure consciousness and then progressively enveloped themselves in denser and denser energy bodies in order to operate at lower and lower frequencies, all the way down to the physical. Although there is some speculation involved in the nature and naming of these various soul wraps, it seems certain that a return to the Source would involve shedding them in reverse order, and thus living at higher and higher frequencies or "levels" until the Origin is reached.

Whether or not a return to the Source is mandated, desirable, or even possible (you can't come back if you never left) is debatable.

Q. **Before we end this, I have one last question. You stated that your answers are synthesized from numerous sources. Are all your sources in 100-percent agreement?**

A. No.

There are some differences in the details reported. Frankly, I'd be surprised if there weren't. For one thing, as we discussed last evening on the way to dinner, discarnate entities have not been goof-proofed. Neither are they all-knowing (at least not the ones available for conversations with us Earthlings), nor are they necessarily immune from natural human tendencies to speculate beyond their current knowledge. For another thing, the truth may not be the same in all the various realities that make up the totality of God's being.

Nevertheless, the reports sent back from beyond death's door are sufficiently consistent on important matters to provide a high degree of confidence in the mosaic we have been assembling.

Sunday Lunch

Why This Could Be

The stream of knowledge is heading towards a non-mechanical reality; the universe begins to look more like a great thought than a great machine.

— Astrophysicist Sir James Jeans,
The Mysterious Universe, p. 148.

It had been a long and intense morning, so most of our lunch was spent resting and refueling. Towards the end, however, we dove briefly but deeply into the meaning of what we had spent the weekend discussing. Here, as best as I could reconstruct it, is our conversation on why God created the universe and what man's role in it is. Please note that neither I nor the old man pretend any special knowledge of, connection to, or revelation from the Almighty Creator. The concepts presented herein are those revealed by discarnate souls or deduced from their revelations.[119]

I believe I had made some rather awkward statement about the purpose of life when he said to me:

"Have you ever considered the conundrum of omnipotent desire?"

"You mean, if God is perfect, He cannot lack anything; therefore He cannot desire anything?"

"Exactly."

"And without desire," I continued, "there could be no motivation for God to make the rather stupendous effort necessary to create the universe."

"Very good," he gave me one of his charming but all too rare grins, "but imagine, if you will, that you have spent most of the last 5 years in a gym developing your chest and arm muscles."

"Oooookay," I replied, raising my eyebrows just a bit, "I don't know if my imagination is up to such an outlandish idea, but I'll try."

"Well, challenge it a bit more by imagining that one day you and your super-sized chest are walking down the street and, because you aren't used to being so wide, you bump into a man and knock him to the ground. Turns out this man is really a dark wizard. (I dare not say his name.) He becomes very angry, pulls out his wand and zaps you."

---

[119] See Walsch, pp. 21-28; Knight, p. 79; Roberts, *The Seth Material*, pp. 240-244; TenDam, p. 285; Newton, *Destiny of Souls*, p. 132.

"Ouch!"

"Not only 'ouch,' but you suddenly find that you can hardly move your arms. You look down and confirm that all your muscles are still there, but you barely have the strength of an infant. You see, the wizard is also psychic and he knows how upset you'll be to have great strength but be prevented from experiencing the use of that strength."

"It's difficult to think of 'having' anything if you can't make use of it," I agreed.

"And, just as there is no value in being extremely strong if you cannot experience the exercise of that strength, so there is no value in being extremely wise if you can never experience the application of your wisdom. Likewise, no joy ensues from perfect love without experiencing the process of loving. The characteristics generally attributed to God — omniscience, omnipotence, over-arching compassion, etc — are of no consequence without a mechanism of experiencing their employment.

"You see, there is one thing, and only one thing that Perfect Allness lacks, that it *must* lack, by definition, and that is an outside viewpoint. If God is all, than God cannot 'see himself as others see him' because there *are* no others.

"The key word is 'separateness.' God, the Universal Mind, The Prime Force, All That Is — by virtue of being God — lacks that separate viewpoint that is necessary to *experience* being God."

"So, you're saying that God's purpose for the universe is to enable God to experience being God."

"I can't imagine any other. And from that" he continued, "we can extrapolate with fair assurance that each soul, being a tiny bit of God, inherits a like purpose: to experience that small section of the universe that is available to it. We humans are some of the mechanisms employed to have these experiences. Or, to phrase it another way, we are experiential parts of God."

"Most teachers who speak of mankind's purpose put it in terms of 'meeting challenges,' 'fulfilling karma,' or 'learning lessons.' How do such activities mesh with this experiential purpose?"

"Well, it's only natural that teachers see the world in terms of learning something, just as politicians think in terms of righting wrongs and priests are biased in favor of connecting with God. But, God is an explorer, not a prospector."

I must have looked puzzled at this, for he continued, "By that I mean there is no particular experience God is seeking, all the experiences He has are valuable to Him. So, as far as I can tell, our physical world is neither school, prison, nor temple. We are not here to learn, nor to be rehabilitated, nor to worship."

"Just to experience?"

"To *create* and experience. But don't say 'just.' This is the most important job there is, for it is getting to know God. Or, at least, it is one way for God to experience a little bit of Himself."

Then we once again provided God with the experience of clearing the table and washing the dishes.

Sunday Afternoon

Goodbye and Best Evidence

I know how weighty the word "fact" is in science, and I say without hesitation that individual personal continuance is to me a demonstrated fact.
— Sir Oliver Lodge[120]

I put my overnight case in my truck and returned to sit beside him on the front stoop and say my goodbyes. When I eased down next to him he handed me a cold can of Coke and said:

"Did my little course meet with your expectations?"

I told him I thought it was excellent and most convincing, then added: "The only thing I foresaw that didn't happen was me staring into the flickering fire while you told hair-raising tales of haunted houses and spectral encounters."

"I suppose a bit more atmosphere wouldn't hurt," he replied. "I'll have to consider adding a ghost

---

[120] Lodge, *Why I Believe in Personal Immortality*, p. 1

story or two. Trouble is, those tales that cause the most shivers are rarely well documented, while the more evidential accounts seem rather mundane."

"Then you don't think that they're all hallucinations?"

"Oh no. There are numerous cases with multiple witnesses, both sequentially and simultaneously. These witnesses report observing the identical locations, clothing, actions, and expressions. Some ghosts have been seen head-on by those facing it and in left and right profile by those standing to either side.[121] Of course, some reports of ghosts probably are the results of hallucination, but all or even most reports certainly cannot be so easily explained away."

"Just how *would* you explain ghost sightings?"

"As I said yesterday, I cannot say for certain how any part of this old world actually works; but, I can most easily imagine the phenomenon as a matter of bleed-through caused by an overlapping of twinks. The majority of sightings don't demonstrate life after death so much as *energy* after death."[122]

"Any final questions before you hit the road?"

"I think you've pretty well covered the subject," I said, "but there is one thing that concerns me a bit."

"And that is?"

"How can I be certain that I will be me? After I die, that is."

---

[121] Gauld, pp. 238-239.

[122] See Myers, p. 209.

"Imagine that we have the power to reach back in time and find you as you were at the age of 7," he said, "and that we magically transport that 7-year-old you onto this porch right now."

"Okay."

"We'll calm him down, and give him a soda, and sit him right there next to you. Then we look him over carefully and have a little chat with him."

"You know, I don't recall anything like that happening to me."

Ignoring my feeble attempt at humor, he continued: "In this *imaginary* situation, I have super x-ray vision. I can see the finest structures of this boy's body, and of yours. After careful comparison, I can attest that not a single molecule is the same. Over the years separating the two of you, your body has totally changed. And, in talking with the boy, I am hard pressed to discover any non-physical similarities between him and the person I know to be you. Your voices are different, as is your vocabulary. Your outlook on life … virtually every aspect of who you are today seems markedly different from the 7-year-old version of yourself. Indeed, should a stranger walk up the drive and speak at length with you both, she would never suspect any link beyond a slight familial resemblance."

"But we'd have the same memories of being a child."

"You think so? You'd be surprised how much your memories have morphed over the years."

"You're probably right," I mused. "I was watching *The Wizard of Oz* with my grandson Dylan the other night, and I kept thinking they must have changed the movie, because I remembered it being different."

"Now," he went on, "you didn't die as a young man ..."

"Not that I recall."

"Yet, in most every way we can measure, the you that was 7 years old no longer exists.

"Just as you did not mourn his passing, so you need not be concerned about future life changes. Memories become muddled and faded, but our sense of self continues to grow stronger. All of the evidence we have points to the next life being most joyous and satisfying.

"Do you remember dreams?"

""Sometimes when I first wake up I do. But only the most recent one, and only for a moment," I replied. "Very few make a lasting impression."

"Have you ever been going about your daily business when some small event — some piece of conversation overheard or some action or scene observed — triggered the sudden recall of a dream? Not one of the dreams you ever remembered, but one you never knew you had dreamed until that moment. And you are a bit startled, and you think 'Hey, I had a dream about this!' "

"Yeah, that's happened to me a few times. It's a pretty weird feeling."

"So then, you have at least a fleeting familiarity with the experience of realizing that there has been more to your life than you had thought up to that moment. That dream was a part of your previous experience, part of who you were, yet you were going through life without any awareness of it. So," he lifted his eyes directly to mine, "which was the true you?"

I returned his gaze with a befuddled stare.

"You are your memories, are you not?"

I managed to nod and say: "At least partially."

"Then the 'you' that existed before your recall of that dream was at least somewhat different than the 'you' that existed afterwards, because your memories were different. So, at the point you gained the new memory, did you become less 'you'?"

"Well, no," I said, wondering where all this was going. "I was still the same me ... maybe just a tiny bit more."

"Indeed. And a similar feeling awaits you on the other side of this life. Soon after your body's death you will wake up to the memory of who you really are, and your reaction will be a mixture of relief and consternation. You'll exclaim things like 'Oh, wow ... of course! ... How could I have forgotten all of that?' Then, you will realize how much more of 'you' you are.

"And at some point in the far future, that greater 'you' will move on to another plane of existence and you will meet up with even more of 'you.' And once again you will be taken by surprise and feel chagrined to remember that larger self that you really are. And so the process will go on and on through successive stages, at each of which you will realize a continually grander 'you.'"

"Are you saying that I will merge with other souls?" I asked.

"I am saying that you will come to remember that you and other souls are, and always have been, one soul. That you will overcome the forgetfulness that now makes you feel separate and alone.

"I will be going through the same process, of course. And there will come a time when we will both remember that we are each other. Then we'll recall, fondly I hope, this conversation we once had with ourself.

"You will never be less than you are right now. There will never be any diminishment of your current personality, no loss of any sense of self ... just continued merging with more and more parts of you, gaining more and more memories, until, at long last, all of our journeys are complete. Until we remember being All That Is.

"Even when you become God again, you will still remember being you."

For awhile I could think of nothing to say, so I just sat there in the sunlight letting his words sink in. Then, I realized there was nothing more I could say, so I stood and grasped his hand. "Thank you so much for an enlightening weekend. Now that I've got a book-full of the most convincing evidence for Survival, I feel a bit less anxious about dying."

"Don't expect to ever get over that anxiety completely," he said, shaking my hand warmly. "The human animal you reside within will never 'go gentle into that good night,'[123] it was programmed to keep itself physically alive, else we wouldn't be standing here today.

"I'll tell you a secret about that book, though. In my opinion, the very best, most convincing evidence isn't in there."

Now, *that* got my attention real good. "Why would you hold out on me?" I stammered. "Are you saving the best for another weekend?"

"Oh no. I'm not holding out on you. The very best evidence isn't one colossal case that would suffice as proof to everyone; the best evidence is an amalgam of millions of personal incidents.

"Polls show that most people believe in life-after-death and in some sort of heaven.[124] Much of this belief is based on personal experience. Almost everyone could tell a story about themselves or some member of their family that suggests the reality of an afterlife. We don't generally hear these stories unless we probe for them and, by themselves,

---

[123] Thanks to Dylan Thomas for that memorable phrase.

[124] Gallup, pp. 139 & 143.

they rarely rate publication.[125] But if you could stand back and grasp the huge volume of experiences, you'd see that the evidence is overwhelming.

"And, we should not forget the work of the many hundreds of unheralded but talented psychics out there. Most are honest, sincere, and dedicated to helping souls on both sides communicate with one another."

"Having been convinced by the major cases you've shown me," I said, "I'll certainly be more open to such less prominent stories in the future."

"As well you should. But don't go to the extreme and blindly accept every story and claim that you hear either. The certainty that there really is a spiritual or astral plane populated by living souls does not negate the fact that some souls, both here and there, are liars and frauds who seek to drain your energy or your wallet. As they go about making their own hell, don't let them come between you and heaven.

"Be open to the spirit, but don't disengage your critical mind."

"Sounds like excellent advice," I said, starting my truck and putting it in gear. "Be assured, I shall try to follow it." I thanked him again, and he wished me a safe journey, and I drove off down the tree-shadowed drive.

---

[125] See www.thesurvivalfiles.com for lists of books describing such experiences. Also, many of these stories have been published in the "My Proof of Survival" columns of *Fate* magazine.

The last glimpse I caught of him, in my "magic" rear-view mirror, he was throwing a stick for Dasher to retrieve.

As I headed towards my in-law's to pick up my wife and continue our vacation, I began to recap the weekend. Of course, I had my recordings and the *Afterlife Casebook*, so I knew I had a lot of reviewing and analyzing and writing time ahead. (In fact, it took almost a year to put it all together.) Nevertheless, I couldn't help considering what, of all the great evidence I had received, was the most convincing. Then, while sitting at a traffic light and weighing which route to take, it occurred to me that pieces of evidence are very like paths to a destination — which one is best depends upon where you start out.

Since each reader had his or her own beliefs when they came to this book, there isn't likely to be a consensus on what evidence is strongest. Obviously, I thought all the cases were worthy of inclusion, and these are only a small portion of the evidential material that has been collected over the past few decades. Perhaps the children's near-death experiences had the greatest affect on you, or the OBEs of people blind since birth. I will always remember the malefic goldsmith and his abused apprentice; but, all things considered, the buried crosses impressed me most.

I trust that you have been equally impressed, and thus reassured by these 23 cases.

The "Old Man" and I look forward to meeting you in this life or the next.

Appendix One

Worthwhile Websites

Sites for this book:
>All the links and books listed below are available from these sites, plus much more.
>**http://www.thesurvivalfiles.com**
>**http://www.momentpointmedia.com**

The following are listed in alphabetical order. Sites that the general reader may find most interesting and useful are marked with a ★.

The Academy of Religion and Psychical Research
>http://www.lightlink.com/arpr

American Society for Psychical Research
>http://www.aspr.com

The Archives of Scientists' Transcendent Experiences (TASTE)
>http://www.issc-taste.org

Association for Skeptical Investigation
>http://www.skepticalinvestigations.org/home.htm

Forever Family Foundation
>http://www.foreverfamilyfoundation.org/

★ Instrumental Transcommunication
http://www.worlditc.org

International Association for Near-Death Studies
http://iands.org/

★ The International Survivalist Society
http://www.survivalafterdeath.org

★ A Lawyer Presents the Case for the Afterlife
http://www.victorzammit.com

Near Death Experience Research Foundation
http://www.nderf.org

The Society for Psychical Research
http://www.spr.ac.uk

The Society for Scientific Exploration
http://www.scientificexploration.org/

Stevenson, Greyson, Alvarado, etc. at UVA
http://www.healthsystem.virginia.edu/internet
/personalitystudies/

Appendix Two

Glossary
Terms and Acronyms as Used Herein

anomaly: An action, event, or result that is unexpected according to conventional scientific knowledge. Something that doesn't fit the established pattern.

apparition: The seeming appearance in one's presence of a person or animal (deceased or living) and related objects such as clothing and vehicles, that are in fact out of one's normal sensory range. A ghost.

astral: A plane or place of existence other than the physical yet near enough to the physical so that actions in one may influence actions in the other. Often used as a synonym for heavenly or spiritual.

control: An entity who acts as liaison between spirits and the sitters through an entranced medium. Some controls claim to be independent spirits, while others say they are portions of the oversoul containing the medium.

corporeal: Characterized by physicality. Bodily.

cross-correspondences: A complex series of independent communications delivered to two or more geographically separate mediums such that the complete message is not clear until the separate fragments are combined into a meaningful whole.

discarnate: Not in a physical body.

doppelganger: An apparitional double or counterpart of a living person.

ethereal: Non-physical. Airy. Celestial.

EVP: Electronic Voice Phenomena. Sounds said to be the voices of deceased individuals, recorded on magnetic tape.

ghost: The apparition of a deceased person or animal. Also used to denote a soul that remains bound to the physical world after the death of its body.

incarnate: Residing in a physical body.

LBL: Life Between Lives. A reference to the activities of a soul when in-between earthly lives, *i.e.*, in heaven.

medium: A person whose mind is capable of acting as a bridge for the exchange of information between discarnate and incarnate souls.

NDA: Nearing Death Awareness. Visions and other sensations of discarnate activity experienced by persons approaching death.

NDE: Near Death Experience. Activities of a person's soul during unconsciousness, recalled after a close brush with bodily death.

OBE [OOBE]: Out-Of-Body Experience. (Herein called Other-Body Experience.) Perception of things and events while the body is sleeping, entranced, or comatose, accompanied by a feeling of being outside of the body.

oversoul: A speculative greater soul, of which a particular soul is but one part.

para [-normal, -psychology, -physics, or whatever]: From the Greek for "beyond" or "beside."

psi: Psychic, psychical, or parapsychological phenomena. Actions and effects not understandable in terms of accepted physics and psychology. [From the Greek "psyche" (pronounced SIGH-key) meaning "soul" or "mind."]

reincarnation: The system, process, or doctrine involving the living of successive physical lives by a soul. [Also termed metempsychosis, palingenesis, re-birth, re-embodiment, and transmigration.]

revenant: The physical manifestation of the return, in whole or in part, of a discarnate soul. A ghost.

soul: A bit of spirit that possesses self-awareness and free will. A mechanism by which God experiences being Himself.

spirit: God stuff. Essence of Creator. Often used as a synonym for soul. Sometimes indicates the non-physical (even though the physical must be formed of the spirit, for there is no other source).

Appendix Three

References Consulted
And Readings Recommended

All of these have some value to the serious student of psychic phenomena and Survival. For recommended readings, see TheSurvivalFiles.com.

For ease in locating copies of books, I have included the International Standard Book Numbers (ISBN) for available editions. These numbers may not always match the publisher of the editions I referenced. The dates given are the original copyright dates.

Alvarado, Carlos S. Ph.D., "The Concept of Survival of Bodily Death and the Development of Parapsychology," *Journal of the Society for Psychical Research*, Volume 67.2, Number 871, April 2003.

Berger, Arthur S., *Aristocracy of the Dead*, McFarland & Co., 1987, ISBN: 0899502598.

Bernstein, Morey, *The Search for Bridey Murphy*, Doubleday & Co.,1965, ISBN: 0385260032.

Brinkley, Dannion, *Saved by the Light*, Villard Books, 1994, ISBN: 0679431764.

Braude, Stephen, "Out-of-Body Experiences and Survival After Death," *International Journal of Parapsychology*, Volume 12, Number 1, 2001, pp. 83-129.

Callanan, Maggie and Patricia Kelley, *Final Gifts*, Poseidon Press, 1992, ISBN: 0553378767.

Carington, Whately, *Telepathy, An Outline of Its Facts, Theory and Implications*, Creative Age Press, 1946.

Cerminara, Gina, *Many Mansions*, New American Library, 1950, ISBN: 068802050X.

Cox-Chapman, Mally, *The Case for Heaven*, G.P. Putnam's Sons, 1995, ISBN: 1559497017.

Crenshaw, James, *Telephone Between Worlds*, DeVorss & Co., 1950, ISBN: 087516692X.

Coover, John E., "Metapsychics and the Incredulity of Psychologists," in *The Case For and Against Psychical Belief*, edited by Carl Murchison, Clark University Press, 1927.

Eadie, Betty J., and Curtis Taylor, *Embraced by the Light*, Gold Leaf Press, 1992. ISBN: 1882723007.

Ebbern, Hayden, Sean Mulligan, and Barry Beyerstein, "Maria's Near-Death Experience: Waiting for the Other Shoe to Drop," *Skeptical Inquirer*, July/August 1996.

Ebon, Martin, *The Evidence for Life After Death*, New American Library, 1977, ISBN: 0451075439.

Edwards, Paul, "The Case Against Reincarnation," Parts 1-4, *Free Inquiry*, Fall 1986-Summer 1987.

Estep, Sarah Wilson, *Voices of Eternity*, Ballentine Books, 1988, ISBN: 0449134245.

Ford, Arthur, and Margueritte Harmon Bro, *Nothing So Strange*, Paperback Library, 1958/1968.

_____, as told to Jerome Ellison, *The Life Beyond Death*, G.P. Putnam's Sons, 1971, ISBN: 0425034224.

Fuller, John G., *The Ghost of 29 Megacycles*, New American Library, 1981. ISBN: 0451143051.

Garland, Hamlin, *Forty Years of Psychic Research*, The MacMillan Co., 1937.

_____, *The Mystery of the Buried Crosses*, E.P. Dutton & Co., 1939.

Gauld, Alan, *Mediumship and Survival: A Century of Investigations*, Paladin Books, 1983, ISBN: 0586084290.

Goldberg, Bruce, *Past Lives, Future Lives*, Ballentine Books, 1982, ISBN: 034535575X.

Grosso, Michael, "Afterlife Research and the Shamanic Turn," *Journal of Near-Death Studies*, Fall 2001, vol. 20, p. 1.

Hodgson, Richard, "A Further Record of Observations of Certain Phenomena of Trance," *The Proceedings of the Society for Psychical Research*, 1897-8, Vol. 13, pp. 284-582.

Homewood, Harry, *Thavis Is Here*, Fawcett, 1978, ISBN: 0449139913

Hyslop, James, *Science and a Future Life*, G.P. Putnam's Sons, 1906.

Huxley, Laura, *This Timeless Moment: A Personal View of Aldous Huxley*, Celestial Arts, 1968, ISBN: 0890879680.

Jung, Carl Gustave, *Memories, Dreams, Reflections*, Random House/Pantheon, 1963. ISBN: 0679723951.

Keene, M. Lamar, *The Psychic Mafia*, Dell Publishing Co., 1976, ISBN: 1573921610.

Knight, J.Z., *Ramtha*, Sovereignty, 1986, ISBN: 0932231113.

Kübler-Ross, Elisabeth, *On Death and Dying*, Macmillan Publishing Co., 1969, ISBN: 0684839385.

Lodge, Sir Oliver, *The Survival of Man*, Methuen, 1909.

_____, *Raymond, or Life and Death*, George H. Doran Co., 1916.

_____, *Why I Believe in Personal Immortality*, Methuen, 1928.

Mathes, J.H., and Lenora Huett, *The Amnesia Factor*, Celestial Arts, 1975, ISBN: 0890870233.

McRae, Ron, *Mind Wars*, St. Martin's Press, 1984, ISBN: 0312652313.

Meek, George W., *After We Die, What Then?*, Metascience Corporation, 1980, ISBN: 0935436006.

_____, "Spiricom: Electronic Communications with the 'Dearly Departed'!" *New Realities* magazine, Vol IV, No. 6, July 1982.

Miller, R. DeWitt, *You DO Take It With You*, The Citadel Press, 1955.

Monroe, Robert, *Journeys Out of the Body*, Doubleday & Co., 1971. ISBN: 0385008619.

_____, *Far Journeys*, Doubleday & Co., 1985. ISBN: 0385231814.

Montgomery, Ruth, *A Search for the Truth*, Bantam Books, 1967, ISBN: 0449210855.

Moody, Raymond, Jr., *Life After Life*, Mockingbird Books, 1975. ISBN: 0553100807.

_____, *Reflections on Life After Life*, Mockingbird Books, 1977. ISBN: 055311140X.

_____, *The Light Beyond*, Bantam Books, 1988. ISBN: 0553278134.

_____, *Coming Back*, Bantam Books, 1991. ISBN: 0553070592.

_____, *Reunions*, Villard Books, 1993. ISBN: 0679425705.

Morehouse, David, *Psychic Warrior*, St. Martin's Press, 1996, ISBN: 0312147082.

Morse, Melvin, and Paul Perry, *Closer to the Light*, Ivy Books, 1990. ISBN: 0804108323.

Moss, Thelma, *The Probability of the Impossible*, J.P. Tarcher, 1974, ISBN: 0874770254.

Myers, F.W.H., *Human Personality and its Survival of Bodily Death*, (first published in 1903) single volume edition published in 1961, University Books.

Netherton, Morris, and Nancy Shiffrin, *Past Lives Therapy*, William Morrow & Co., 1978.

Newton, Michael, *Journey of Souls*, fifth revised edition, Llewellyn Publications, 1996. ISBN: 1567184855.

_____, *Destiny of Souls*, Llewellyn Publications, 2000, ISBN: 1567184995.

Osis, Karlis and Erlendur Haraldsson, *What They Saw ... At the Hour of Death*, Hastings House, 1997, ISBN: 0803893868.

Pole, Wellesley Tudor, *Private Dowding: The personal story of a soldier killed in battle*, Clarke, Doble, and Brendon, Ltd., 1917.

Price, Harry, *Leaves from a Psychist's Case-Book*, Victor Gollancz, 1933.

_____, *Fifty Years of Psychical Research: A Critical Survey*, Longmans, Green & Co., 1939.

Radin, Dean, *The Conscious Universe: The Scientific Truth of Psychic Phenomena*, HarperCollins Publishers, 1997, ISBN: 0062515020.

Randles, Jenny, and Peter Hough, *The Afterlife*, Berkley Books, 1993, ISBN: 0425142124.

Rieder, Marge, *Mission to Millboro*, Blue Dolphin Press, 1991, ISBN: 0931892597.

_____, *Return to Millboro*, Blue Dolphin Press, 1996, ISBN: 0931892287.

Ring, Kenneth, and Evelyn Valarino, *Lessons from the Light*, Moment Point Press, 1998. ISBN: 0966132785.

_____, and Sharon Cooper, *Mindsight: Near-Death and Out-of-Body Experiences in the Blind*, William James

Center for Consciousness Studies, 1999, ISBN: 0966963008.

Roberts, Jane, *The Seth Material*, Prentice-Hall, 1970, ISBN: 0138071802.

_____, *Seth Speaks*, Bantam Books, 1972, ISBN: 1878424076.

Schmicker, Michael, *Best Evidence*, 2nd Ed., Writer's Club Press, 2002, ISBN: 0595219063.

Schwartz, Gary, with William L. Simon, *The Afterlife Experiments*, Pocket Books, 2002.

Sharp, Kimberly Clark, *After the Light*, William Morrow & Co., 1995. ISBN: 0688137644.

Smith, Alson J., *Immortality: The Scientific Evidence*, NAL/Signet, 1954.

Snow, Robert L., *Looking for Carroll Beckwith*, Rodale Books, 1999. ISBN: 1579541011.

Spraggett, Allen, *The Unexplained*, Signet Mystic Books / New American Library, Inc., 1967.

_____, with William V. Rauscher, *Arthur Ford: The Man Who Talked with the Dead*, New American Library, 1973.

Steiger, Brad, *Mysteries of Time and Space*, Dell Publishing Company, 1974, ISBN: 0440059240.

Stevenson, Ian, *The Evidence for Survival from Claimed Memories of Former Incarnations*, M.C. Peto, 1961.

Sugrue, Thomas, *There Is a River: The Story of Edgar Cayce*, Dell Publishing Co., 1942, ISBN: 0876043759.

Talbot, Michael, *The Holographic Universe*, HarperCollins, 1991, ISBN: 0060922583.

TenDam, Hans, *Exploring Reincarnation*, Rider Books, 2003, ISBN: 0712660208.

Tymn, Michael, "The Mystery of the Buried Crosses," *Fate*, March, 2005, pp. 12-19.

_____, "The Return of Sir William Barrett," *Fate*, October, 2005, pp. 50-55.

Walsch, Neale Donald, *Conversations With God, Book. I*, G.P. Putnam's Sons, 1995, ISBN: 0399142789.

Wambach, Helen, *Life Before Life*, Bantam Books, 1979, ISBN: 0553124501.

White, Stewart Edward, *The Betty Book*, E.P. Dutton & Co., 1937, ISBN: 0525474471.

_____, and Harwood White, *Across the Unknown*, E.P. Dutton & Co., 1939.

_____, *The Unobstructed Universe*, E.P. Dutton & Co., 1940. ISBN: 0525470425.

Wilson, Colin, *Afterlife*, Doubleday & Company, 1985, ISBN: 0385237669.

WHO SHOULD READ THIS document. If you are interested in, concerned with, endorse, or question the use of the scientific approach in psi investigations or the goal of finding scientific proof of psychic phenomena, then you may wish to read this document. Essentially, it argues that the scientific method is inappropriate for investigating psychic events due, in part, to the impossibility of controlling all factors, and that legal concepts of proof and good detective work are indicated in its place.

Appendix Four

The Scientific Fallacy

Ruminations on Psi Research and Reviews
by Miles Edward Allen

Evidence in science is always a matter of degree ... Both critics and proponents need to learn to think of adjudication in science as more like that found in the law courts, imperfect and with varying degrees of proof and evidence.

— Marcello Truzzi
"On Pseudo-Skepticism," the *Zetetic Scholar*, #12-13.

Carl Sagan, whom I greatly admired as a concerned and public-spirited astronomer, once asked: "How is it, that channelers never give us verifiable information otherwise unavailable?"[1]

Other than the biased way in which Sagan's question is phrased (*i.e.* the assumption that they *don't* give such information), there are several difficulties here. The main one, as you should realize by now, is that channelers *have* provided information unknown to anyone living at the time, yet subsequently verified. Garland's buried crosses, the Cayce oil-of-smoke incident, and the Millboro underground railroad are a few that come to mind immediately. But besides revealing his ignorance of psychic phenomena, Sagan's comments demonstrate several common problems with the so-called "scientific" approach.

On first hearing it, the concept of "verifiable information otherwise unavailable" sounds reasonable enough, but a closer examination reveals an extremely tough, if not impossible, criterion. "Information otherwise unavailable" would have to be information <u>proven not to exist</u> in any person's mind or in any library or any other place in the world! And since, as skeptics are so fond of pointing out, "it is impossible to prove a negative," this proof is unattainable. No matter how hard one tried, one could never be sure that the information was not available somewhere.

As if this wasn't obstacle enough, Sagan also wants the information to be "verifiable." Just how, do you suppose, is it possible to verify information that doesn't exist?

Let's look at one of the examples he offers in elaborating his query. "Why does Alexander the Great never tell us about the exact location of his tomb?"

Suppose that a psychic did meet with professor Sagan and channeled Alexander, who revealed his tomb's location precisely enough for an archeological team to dig it up. Based on the history of the scientific community's reaction to phenomena that do not fit in their world view, we can be sure that such a series of events would change the minds of very few scientists, and of no professional skeptics. Instead of "Wow, channeling is a real phenomenon!" we would have a chorus of lettered men and women claiming:

(1) that the location of the tomb must have been in some document seen by the channeler, or

(2) that the channeler actually 'saw' the tomb clairvoyantly, or

(3) that the channeler precognitively saw the future discovery of the tomb, or

(4) that the location of the tomb was pulled from the "collective unconscious," or

(5) that Sagan and the channeler are frauds who made up the story after the tomb was discovered.

If you think this last option too outlandish, you don't know how fast scientists can turn on a brother, no matter how well respected. Had he endorsed the channeler, the esteemed professor would have been ostracized faster than you can say "Crackpot Carl."

And how might Sagan have reacted to the tomb's discovery? A strong clue is in his next paragraph, in which he says: "If some good evidence for life after death were announced, I'd be eager to examine it; but it would have to be real scientific data, not mere anecdote."

Whenever skeptics demand that psychic evidence be "scientific," they mean that it must come from replicable experiments, perfectly designed and perfectly controlled. Of course, they are well aware that no experiment of any kind has ever been perfect and so they will always have a way of discrediting evidence that doesn't fit their view of things. And even if it were "good" evidence based on "real scientific data," Sagan does not suggest that he would accept it, only that he would "examine it."

Scientists also know that psychic phenomena in general and spirit communication in particular do not lend themselves well to repeatable laboratory experimentation. For example, the main reason that Alexander hasn't revealed the location of his tomb is probably that he has better things to do than try to communicate with skeptical scientists.

Not only does Sagan require this scientific evidence, he goes further and rules out the acceptance of "mere anecdote." Now, an "anecdote" is a brief account of an interesting incident; therefore, Sagan is setting up a dichotomy: either evidence is "real scientific data" or it must be treated as just another story or fable. Note that he leaves no room for testimony. No matter how many nor how prestigious the witnesses to the interesting incident, no matter what oath is taken under what penalty, all testimony is relegated to folklore unless the incident can be repeated in a laboratory or seen through a scope.

The Irrepressible Spirits

The key difficulty in trying to apply the scientific method to the investigation of paranormal abilities and events is the impossibility of controlling all the parameters, especially the ethereal ones.

The work of Dr. Schwartz as detailed in *The Afterlife Experiments* provides excellent examples of this problem,

I focus on Schwartz' work because it is some of the best ever done, not because it is uniquely susceptible to the problems — which are endemic to all "scientific" research in the field.

Schwartz reports that after several of the readings by the psychics, lists of possible statements were shown to students acting as a control group, who attempted to guess what statements might apply to the sitter. In normal scientific research, control groups are gatherings of people who are not involved with or affected by the object of investigation. For instance, if the study concerns the effects of a certain pill, the control group would consist of folks who have never taken the pill. But in researching psychical abilities, the attributes being studied cannot be assumed to be limited to the test group. If any personality survives death, it is very likely (although not absolutely certain) that *every* personality survives death. If anyone can receive messages from discarnate beings, than it is highly probable that *everyone* can receive messages from discarnate beings, to some extent or another. Such universal potentials make it impossible to isolate a control group from the phenomena being studied. All that Schwartz accomplished by creating control groups of this sort was to give skeptics another opportunity for irrelevant criticism.

The same problem applies to the idea (mentioned by Schwartz and endorsed by at least one reviewer) of comparing the psychic's performance to that of a "cold-reader" (someone practiced in making educated guesses based on the sitter's responses and body language). But, consider what might happen if the cold-reader's great grand dad were to take that moment to make his presence known and give a little unsought help. In such a case, truly astounding "guesses" could be made that weren't guesses at all. Such interference from the other side would totally distort the outcome of the test and no one would be the wiser.

The Keene Example

An incident described in the confessions of Lamar Keene[2] provides an excellent example of the problem. No skeptic has ever doubted Keene's claim that he achieved wealth and fame as a trance medium through the use of trickery and fraud. His life was turned completely around, Keene testifies, when he met a woman named Florence Hutchinson who became an inspirational mother figure to him. This woman had traveled from Oklahoma to obtain a reading from Keene at the spiritualist enclave of Camp Chesterfield in Indiana. But she had not made a reservation so, Keene says, his "first inclination was to tell her to get lost ... But she really was a kindly and appealing lady," so he allowed her to take the place of her friend who did have an appointment for the next day.

Keene claims that there is a network of fraudulent mediums around the country who maintain and share files of information on their sitters, and that the files kept at Chesterfield were some of the most extensive anywhere. But, when he went to consult these files, he says, "I found myself stymied. Florence Hutchison had never been to Chesterfield before and there was nothing on her in the files. However, since she looked like such an agreeable sort," Keene decided he could get away with doing a cold reading.

This he did, and things were going fine until Florence requested his help in finding a legal document that had been missing since her husband's death. At first she asked if the document had been taken by a certain cousin of whom she was suspicious. It would have been easy for Keene to say yes and end the inquiry right there, but instead, for reasons unknown to him, he said: "Oh no." Whereupon Florence (speaking to whom she thinks is her departed husband) asks: "Well darling, where is it?"

"There was no way of ducking the question except by pretending to lose trance and to suddenly wake up," Keene writes, but: "Then I said the first thing that came into my head, which was: 'You have a metal file cabinet at home, the portable one, and it has a false top in it. There is a key to the false top in the bottom under some papers. The document is in that false top.'" Keene thought that this sounded rather lame, but at least it did get rid of the woman — not for long, however. Florence rushed home to Oklahoma and, as you have probably guessed by now, found the missing document just where Keene said it would be.

Now, Florence's mention of her cousin was exactly the kind of clue Keene was searching for in his cold reading, so what prompted him to reject that solution? As for the rest, Keene concludes that it was all an "incredibly lucky" guess. Actually, though, it was a series of four statements that Keene had no way of knowing: (1) that Florence had a portable metal file at home, (2) that the file had a false top, (3) that the key to that top was beneath the papers, and (4) that the missing document was in the false top. Dismissing those four statements — plus the rejection of the cousin's involvement — as an occurrence of stupendous luck is, indeed, not credible.

Remember, also, that this incident proved to be the key to Keene's reformation from fraudulent medium to honest citizen. Thus, we are asked to believe that this once-in-a-lifetime series of lucky guesses *just happened* to occur when the person who could inspire Keene's turnaround *just happened* to unexpectedly take a friend's place in his séance room. I, for one, reject such a long line of coincidences as preposterous. It is far more reasonable to conclude that Keene had a real psychic experience when he most needed one, especially in light of all the other evidence in favor of spirit contact.

[Note that Keene was hardly the first to lead distraught widows to secret compartments holding important papers. As far back as the mid 1700s, the great scientist and mystic Emanuel Swendenborg did the same.[3]]

If spirits can interfere with a cold reading by an admittedly phoney medium, they can certainly influence cold-readings done as adjuncts to scientific experiments just as they can assist the folks in experimental control groups in making "guesses." **You simply cannot remove the influence of the dead upon the living.**

Counting Blanks

Dead folks are also notoriously unreliable. This creates another problem area for scientists researching the paranormal, as is evident in Schwartz' account of a session[4] in which the medium simply drew a blank, receiving no information about the sitter. Logic and fairness would demand that this session be thrown out of the study. Clearly, it is unreasonable to expect there to be a willing spirit hanging around to talk about every sitter every time. But Schwartz counted the sitting as one in which the medium's accuracy was scored at zero percent — just as if the medium had made a series of statements without any hits. Averaging this zero score in with the medium's other scores would seriously lower the medium's overall rating. I do not see a justification for this approach, unless Schwartz was assuming that the work of pulling information from "the great beyond" was being done solely by the medium and did not depend upon the cooperation of a dearly departed. (If such a bias existed, his results are doubly impressive.)

Detectives Needed

Another trouble science has with psi arises from trying to quantify information that is essentially qualitative. Of what value are counts of hits and misses on irrelevant trivia such a pet's initials or whether the diseased organ was a gall bladder or a spleen? Clearly, numbers *do* lie, or, at least, they are subject to biased interpretations. Statistics are designed to smooth over anomalous results; what we need is to *focus on* the anomalies. All the bar charts and derivatives in the world are not as convincing as a single revelation of unique character attested to by unimpeachable witnesses. To help dig up such evidence, I propose that scientists equip their teams not with statisticians, nor with cold-readers, nor magicians, but with good old-fashioned detectives.

As an example of what I mean, let's examine a case related by Dr. Thelma Moss, in her book *The Probability of the Impossible*.[5] Dr. Moss tells of an investigation by her lab that was prompted by a homeowner's complaint that four different guests, on four separate occasions, had reported seeing a man walking about the house — a man who wasn't there. The homeowner, himself, had never seen this "ghost."

According to Moss, she endeavored to be "scientific" about the investigation by having each of the witnesses interviewed separately and the interviews tape recorded. From these, she learned that each witness reported seeing a man in dark pants and a white shirt (one witness included a suit jacket) walking in and around the house — one witness saw the apparition by a bedroom door, one by the swimming pool, and two saw it walking into the dining room. Next, Moss arranged for six psychics and six "non-psychics" to be given an individual tour of the house, after which they marked on maps any places where they sensed a ghost. Dr. Moss does not include the entire study in her book, but she does make note of "the sophisticated statistical analysis" made of the data. I can just imagine the skeptics tearing that sophisticated analysis to shreds — and, of course, never mentioning the astounding facts buried beneath.

A good detective, searching for proof "beyond reasonable doubt," would pursue this case quite differently. The first step is to go to great lengths to discover if the witnesses were telling the truth when they claimed they did not know one another. This would include full background checks, interviews with friends and neighbors, and perhaps even some stake-outs If any signs of collusion (or even communication) are discovered, then the evidence would be irrevocably contaminated and the investigation discontinued. At the same time, an investigation is needed as to whether or not any of the witnesses have a history of hallucinations or psychoses or have a reputation for playing practical jokes or telling tall tales.

The next item on our detective's agenda is to investigate the possibility that the homeowners had shared one witness' experience with any of the other witnesses, or had encouraged or prompted witnesses in any way (including supplying them with hallucinatory drugs). This would involve further interviews of the witnesses, and the homeowners, and any household help, and close neighbors. Also a full background check on the homeowners is in order to see if they have reported, or been involved in, this sort of incident in the past.

When all the interviews and background checks are done, if he has uncovered no evidence of false testimony, our detective has little choice but to declare the facts valid as reported. In other words, it can be concluded <u>beyond a reasonable doubt</u> that the witnesses actually saw the figure of a man in dark pants and white shirt walking about the house.

Next, our detective considers alternative possibilities for the sightings, the first being hallucination. From our "legal" point-of-view, one witness alone is worthless. She might have actually seen a ghost, but she might be hallucinating due to mental illness, or drugs, or fatigue, or some unknown reason. The likelihood of two witnesses sharing the same hallucination at different times, however, is too incredible to consider. So hallucination can be ruled out in this case.

Unless of course, there really was a stranger present, and it was the homeowner who was having the negative hallucination that a real person was *not* visible. Negative hallucinations are rare, but can be induced via hypnosis, so our dogged gumshoe needs to explore the possibility that the homeowner is under the influence of a hypnotist. Come to think of it, the same goes for the witnesses, who might have all attended a lounge show by the same stage hypnotist who instructed them to see a ghost the next time they were visiting the homeowner. All of which is extremely unlikely, but easy enough to check.

Another improbable but possible scenario is that some prankster or villain used holographic projection or some other technology to display a realistic, 3-dimensional movie of a man in dark pants and white shirt. Our detective can rule this out, not only because the homeowner did not see the apparition as it "walked swiftly around the pool," but because the incidents took place in three different locations, thereby vastly increasing the difficulty of unobtrusively setting up and dismantling the required equipment.

Assuming that all the interrogations and investigations had been properly done with no adverse results, the "case of the four visitors" could have been one of the most evidential ever reported. Nothing is ever absolutely, 100-percent certain, but it would have been evidential enough to deserve the label "solid proof" that ghosts exist.

The Role of Science

As for the continuation of life after death, it seems clear that experts will never reach a consensus on a statistically sound, scientifically replicable, proof. Not only can statistics always be distorted, but some experimental factors, such as the involvement of discarnate entities, can never be controlled. In my opinion, this does not matter, for the cases presented in this book are more than sufficient to establish proof beyond a reasonable doubt in any court of logical and objective minds.

All this should not be construed to mean that I am some sort of psychic Luddite seeking a return to the days of table tipping in darkened parlors — not without an infrared camera anyway. EMF meters, voice analyzers, EEG machines, and other such technological advances have a definite place in psi research. And science has a valid role in determining the characteristics and factors at play in various phenomena. But, scientists need to stop wasting time and resources on attempts to prove the already proven existence of psychic phenomena and concentrate more on determining how it works.

Notes for *The Scientific Fallacy*

1. *The Demon-Haunted World*, 1995.
2. Keene, chapter 8.
3. Berger, p. 7.
4. Schwartz, p. 187.
5. Moss, p. 323.

Appendix Five

The Skeptical Quagmire
by Miles Edward Allen

Personally I prefer to consider the word of the scientific man who is sacrificing his time, his health and his reputation in the effort to solve a persistent mystery, than the snap judgment of a professional conjurer.

— Hamlin Garland[1]

I've never been comfortable knowing only one side of a story. I insist that my beliefs about an afterlife be based on the best evidence and take into account all the evidence and all the reasonable arguments both for and against that belief. That is why the concept for *The Survival Files* always included a section in which I would present the other side of the issues as objectively and clearly as I could. In pursuit of that goal, I sought the views of the skeptical, the unbeliever, and the agnostic. Much to my dismay, I have found very little worth quoting.

To be sure, there are a few deceitful people ready to relieve you of your purse by faking contact with the spirit world. Some of these villains are so adept at snooping and cold-reading and sleight-of-hand (and foot) that they can fool many of the people much of the time. Thus, in this treacherous world, it is wise to be skeptical. But there are significant differences between being skeptical and being a "professional skeptic" or what I have come to call an "überskeptic" (a term I define as an outspoken proponent of skepticism whose livelihood, power base, and/or social status depends on bolstering the illusion that all psychic phenomena are bogus).

Being skeptical means being aware of the possibility of fraud and coincidence; being an überskeptic means automatically rejecting all possibilities except fraud and coincidence. Being skeptical means remaining open to all possibilities until one is proven to be correct; being an überskeptic means being closed to any psychic explanation, no matter how strong the evidence or how preposterous the other possibilities. Most critically, being skeptical means giving all sides of an issue a fair hearing; being an überskeptic apparently imparts a willingness to mislead others as to the existence and nature of psychic phenomena.

There are a plethora of überskeptics in this world. Many are philosophers, some are scientists, and a surprising number are magicians (or, at least, amateur magicians). Several are such skilled communicators that their influence is widespread. It is very likely that readers of this document have been influenced by the works of these professional naysayers, and so I feel I have a duty to expose their devious methods.

The approach most often and enthusiastically followed to obscure evidence for Survival is to attack the character of either the witness or the researchers who present such claims. Of course, if a witness has been known to fabricate experiences or the researcher known to falsify data, then it is legitimate to take such dishonesties into consideration when evaluating their claims. Even when there is no hint of past or present fraud, however, überskeptics often resort to besmirching the people involved. The stronger and more convincing the evidence, the more the skeptics try to focus attention on irrelevancies such as personality.

Although popular with some in the media — because it makes a good story — I find such name-calling to be divisive and detrimental to the process of understanding and communicating the truth about heaven. Therefore, I shall refrain from using the names of those super skeptical philosophers, scientists, and magicians here. The reader needs to be on the look-out for the tactics I describe herein no matter from whom they originate. And the entrenched überskeptics will know who I am talking about anyway.

Ad Hominem

Since we have already described the focus-on-the-person-not-the-facts approach, I'll start with a few actual examples.

A classic instance of what I call The MacLaine Maneuver (named in honor of dear Shirley, who has been the subject of more skeptics' attempts at humor than any other person) is provided by a long-time critic of the idea of reincarnation. This maneuver involves belittling an idea by poking fun at its proponents. A common way to do that is to suggest that Shirley MacLaine has been in some way associated with them. In attempting to denigrate the past-life regressionist, Dr. Helen Wambach, this critic refers to her as "a star of the tabloids and one of the 'authorities' to whom Shirley MacLaine appeals for a scientific underpinning of her investigation."

Dr. Wambach has done considerable research on people who, under hypnosis, seem to remember past lives. This is similar to the work of the Drs. Goldberg, Netherton, Newton, and many other regression therapists. What really draws this critic's scorn, however, is Wambach's and Goldberg's experiments with progressive hypnosis. He begins his commentary with: "In recent years, past-life regressionists have extended their activities to explorations of future lives." (In fact, the only thing recent is his awareness of the subject; hypnotic progressions have been going on at least since 1910.) He then lampoons the idea, calling Dr. Goldberg a "comedian" of "stupendous talent" and making the MacLaine reference to Dr. Wambach. All this without the slightest mention of any of the mountains of evidence that Goldberg and Wambach have compiled.

Another popular way to imply that people are whackos is to put their name in the same sentence as a reference to UFOs. For instance, when a critic wished to call Dr. Gary Schwartz' character into question — without, of course, risking a libel suit — he wrote: "It might be a warning sign to us that Schwartz was educated at Harvard, which also gave us Dr. John Mack, the man who apparently has never met anyone who hasn't been abducted by space aliens." (The fact that several other überskeptics have also attended Harvard is, naturally, not mentioned.)

Or, observe the not-so-subtle linking in the following comment by another überskeptic: "Unless carefully controlled studies and standards are applied, people can deceive themselves and others into believing that almost anything is true and real — from past-life regression and extraterrestrial abductions to satanic infestations and near-death experiences." Apparently the writer hopes that his readers will be so alienated by aliens or distracted by the devil that they will forget about those cases that *have* been subject to careful controls.

Guilt by Association

Here is a quote from a popular skeptical magazine. The author's statements are technically true — his implications are not.

> "The Society for Psychical Research was founded in 1882 ... These researchers examined reports of apparitions and ghostly hauntings. ... Many famous mediums such as Eusapia Palladino (in Italy) and Leonora Piper (in Boston) were tested under controlled conditions in an effort to determine whether they possessed extraordinary powers.
>
> "Palladino was **especially** elusive, and the scientific community was split as to whether **she** was fraudulent. .... Palladino was also tested in the United States at Harvard by Hugo

Muensterberg (1909) and at Columbia University (1910) by a team of scientists; and in both cases the physical levitation of the table behind her and the feeling of being pinched by her spirit control (called John King) was found to be caused by her adroit ability to stretch her leg in contortions and to pinch sitters with her toes, or levitate a small table behind her. This was detected by having a man dressed in black crawl under the table and see her at work." [Emphasis added.]

The final sentence of the first paragraph quoted is correct — both Palladino and Piper were famous and they were both tested. The next paragraph, detailing some of the tests that Palladino failed, is also accurate — some legitimate questions were raised concerning Palladino's physical effects. But — and this is a huge BUT — Leonora Piper was never, ever accused of cheating by any of those who studied her first hand. As detailed in numerous books and articles, Piper was scrutinized, examined, and analyzed by the most hard-nosed skeptics and the most experienced investigators for decade after decade. One of these skeptical investigators, Professor Richard Hodgson, of Cambridge University, had been a key player in "exposing" Eusapia Palladino and had announced his intention to do likewise to Piper. Not only did he find absolutely no evidence of fraud, but, after 10 years of careful study,[2] Hodgson publicly admitted that he had been wrong and that, in his own words, "I have no hesitation in affirming with the most absolute assurance that the 'spirit' hypothesis is justified by its fruits."[3] He was joined in his endorsement of an afterlife by two other highly respected skeptics who investigated Piper, Professor James Hyslop of Columbia and Professor William James of Harvard.

The material quoted above demonstrates a favored technique that scientism's true believers use to deal with evidence that contradicts their creed – *i.e.*, guilt by association. Since the article's author could say nothing directly against Piper, he introduces her in the same breath as Palladino, hoping that his readers will absorb the unstated but implied idea that both have been discredited. He even says that Palladino "was especially elusive, and the scientific community was split as to whether she was fraudulent," thereby encouraging his readers to infer that, in contrast, Piper was easily exposed and scientists were unanimous in their claims of fraud. (Also, he talks about Palladino pulling tricks in dark rooms, but he fails to mention that Piper worked in rooms that were fully illuminated.)

But the author is not done making unwarranted associations:

> "Late in his career the famous magician Houdini (1874-1926) exposed several bogus mediums. By the 1920s **the spiritualist movement was thoroughly discredited**, because **when the controls were tightened, the effect disappeared**." [Emphasis added.]

In truth, the Spiritualist movement was not discredited during the 1920s; two of the world's best known mediums, Briton Eileen Garrett and American Arthur Ford, were at the height of their careers during the 1930s. Thus, we have here, at best, an opinion stated as a fact. Placing such an opinion immediately after the true (but irrelevant) statement about Houdini, is clearly an attempt to get the reader to falsely assume that Houdini was largely responsible for the exposure of mediums. The final phrase, though — "when the controls were tightened, the effect disappeared" — is simply not true in all cases. With Piper and with others, the controls were tightened and re-tightened to the extreme and the effects just kept on coming.

Amazing Omission

Some debunkers seem quite adept at making relevant facts disappear. Consider, for example, this performance taken from one überskeptic's on-line newsletter.

The critic begins a segment by offering "a few excerpts, with my comments, about a recent news article ..." This article is about Allison Dubois, the psychic who was the model for the TV show *Medium*. He does not give the name of the newspaper, nor the author, nor any citation that might encourage his readers to look at the entire article.[4] He offers a critique of a couple of the minor examples of Dubois' paranormal insights as described in the article. He then dismisses the article and changes the subject.

I must say that this critic did precisely what he said he would do — he offered his comments on a few excerpts. And his criticisms have some merit, although his sarcasm is a bit over the top. The trouble lies in what he did not offer.

The newspaper article from which his excerpts were taken is the very same article that tells the story of Phran

Ginsberg, whose teenage daughter, Bailey, died in a car crash in 2002. Let's take a look at the rest of the story.

Dr. Schwartz had set up a telephone connection between Ginsberg, in New York, and Dubois, in Arizona. Neither party knew the other, and Ginsberg was not allowed to speak. Thus the possibility of prior investigation by the medium was ruled out and educated guesses based on feedback (*i.e.*, cold reading) were impossible.

The article continues:

> The first thing Dubois said was that she saw a photo of her daughter hugging her sister at a party. At that moment, Ginsberg was looking at a photo of the scene.
>
> "Then she told me Bailey wished me 'Happy Valentine's Day.' And that didn't make sense, because it was October," [Ginsberg] said. But later that day, she took the photo from its frame, and on the back Bailey had written 'Valentine's Day Dance.' ...
>
> Dubois also had described the accident and Bailey's fatal head injury.[5]

Describing Bailey's head injury is particularly striking for a reading without feedback, but that could be attributed to mental telepathy. The truly evidential piece, of course, is the reference to information <u>known to no living person</u> — the link between the picture and Valentine's Day.

Whether or not this one account is sufficient proof of life after death is a matter for debate, but when überskeptics bring up only irrelevancies while failing to discuss the really impressive evidence, they do their followers a grave disservice.

False Consensus

This is claiming that most people agree with your position without offering any evidence thereof. Consider, for example, the statement: "Reincarnation may be defined as the view that human beings do not, **as most of us assume**, live only once." This phrase, taken from a series of articles on reincarnation, is both prejudicial and false. The majority of Earth's inhabitants believe in some form of reincarnation and the writer cites no survey of his readership to determine their beliefs in the matter.

Pretended Ignorance

This requires blatantly ignoring all existing evidence in favor of something you reject or against something you embrace. Pointing out that another dimension is not necessary for some views of reincarnation, one professional skeptic wrote that it does not depend on "a mysterious realm whose location cannot be specified and which has never been seen or otherwise observed by anybody." In truth, there is ample testimony from people and spirits who have experienced these realms.

Arguments Not Evidence

In philosophy and mathematics one can prove something by argument alone, but in the real world, proof requires evidence. A thousand lengthy expositions as to why something cannot be are no match for a single citation of that something occurring. Überskeptics often drone on for page after page citing this argument and that argument, all the while refusing to seriously consider any evidence. This is reminiscent of the ancient arguments for the earth being the center of the universe, or the more recent "scientific proofs" that stones cannot fall from the sky.

Incomprehensible Equals Impossible

According to many critics, the most important argument against survival after death is the "body-mind dependence" argument. Many thousands of words have been devoted to various aspects of this argument, but the überskeptics could save us all a lot of eyestrain by condensing their polemics into one simple sentence, to wit: "I don't understand how it could work, therefore it cannot be."

If only they would follow Dr. Jung's lead when that famous psychiatrist stated: "I shall not commit the fashionable stupidity of regarding everything I cannot explain as a fraud."[6]

The idea that "inexplicable equals impossible" is echoed throughout the writings and speeches of überskeptics. Time and again the believer is asked to explain how the mind can survive the death of the brain, or where heaven is located, or why an elderly person's spirit might appear as a younger version of himself, and so on. The answer to all such questions must be "No one knows for sure." But if you are ever faced with such a challenge, you might add that no one knows why electricity works. And no one has ever seen a memory trace in the brain. And, to get down to the real nitty-gritty, no one knows how action-at-a-distance is possible, either. In short, the reality of something is not dependent on our being able to understand it.

God save us from the arrogance of scientists, the condescension of magicians, and the smugness of philosophers!

Notes for *The Skeptical Quagmire*

1. Garland, Hamlin, *Forty Years of Psychic Research*, MacMillan Co., 1937, p. 146.

2. Hodgson studied Piper almost continuously from 1887 until his death in 1905.

3. Hodgson, Richard, "A Further Record of Observations of Certain Phenomena of Trance," *Proceedings of the Society for Psychical Research*, 1897-8, vol. XIII, pp.284-582.

4. Written by Carla McClain and headed "Varied readings on Arizona psychic" the article appeared in the *Arizona Daily Star* on 17 January 2005.

5. Bob Ginsberg, Phran's husband, points out in correspondence with the author that the actual sequence of events was somewhat different than the newspaper article relates (for instance, the statement about the photo was not the first thing Dubois said and Phran did not take the picture from the frame until the next day). Nevertheless, these variations do not affect the strength of the evidence.

6. Carl Gustave Jung, Speech to the SPR, 1919.

Appendix Six

Index

Also by Miles Edward Allen

Christmas Lore & Legend

A holiday trivia game.
"The most fun you can have
without opening presents."

This and other items of interest are available
from Momentpoint Media.
www.momentpointmedia .com